■SCHOLASTIC

GRADE 4

Math Problem-Solving Packets

Mini-Lessons for the Interactive Whiteboard With Reproducible Packets That Target and Teach Must-Know Math Skills

Carole Greenes, Carol Findell & Mary Cavanagh

NEW YORK • TORONTO • LONDON • AUCKLAND • SYDNEY
MEXICO CITY • NEW DELHI • HONG KONG • BUENOS AIRES

Teaching *Resources*

Editor: Maria L. Chang
Cover design by Jorge J. Namerow
Interior design by Melinda Belter
Illustrations by Teresa Anderko

ISBN: 978-0-545-45955-6

1 2 3 4 5 6 7 8 9 10   40   19 18 17 16 15 14 13 12

Table of Contents

Introduction

Welcome to *Math Problem-Solving Packets: Grade 4.* This book is designed to help you introduce students to problem-solving strategies and give them practice in essential number concepts and skills, while motivating them to write and talk about big ideas in mathematics. It also sets the stage for more advanced math learning—algebra, in particular—in the upper grades.

Building Key Math Skills

The National Council of Teachers of Mathematics (NCTM) identifies problem solving as a key process skill and considers the teaching of strategies and methods of reasoning to solve problems a major part of the mathematics curriculum for children of all ages. The Common Core State Standards (CCSS) concurs. "Make sense of problems and persevere in solving them" is the first standard for Mathematical Practice in CCSS.

The problem-solving model first described by renowned mathematician George Polya in 1957 provides the framework for the problem-solving focus of this book. All the problems contained here require students to interpret data displays—such as text, charts, diagrams, graphs, pictures, and tables—and answer questions about them. As they work on the problems, students learn and practice the following problem-solving strategies:

- making lists or cases of possible solutions and testing those solutions
- identifying, describing, and generalizing patterns
- working backward
- reasoning logically
- reasoning proportionally

As students solve the problems in this book, they'll also practice computing, applying concepts of place value and number theory, reasoning about the magnitudes of numbers, and more. In addition, they will learn the "language of mathematics," which includes terminology (e.g., *odd number, variable*) as well as symbols (e.g., >, <). Students will see the language in the problems and illustrations and use the language as they discuss and write about how they solve the problems.

How to Use This Book

This book contains six problem-solving packets—each composed of nine problems featuring the same type of data display (e.g., diagrams, scales, and arrays of numbers)—that focus on one or more problem-solving strategies and algebraic concepts. Each set opens with an overview of the type of problems/tasks in the set, the problem-solving focus, the number concepts or skills needed to solve the problems, the CCSS standard(s) covered, the math language emphasized in the problems, and guiding questions to be used with the first two problems of the packet to help students grasp the key concepts and strategies.

The first two problems in each packet are designed to be discussed and solved in a whole-class setting. The first, "Solve the Problem," introduces students to the type of display and problem they will encounter in the packet. You may want to have students work on this first problem individually or in pairs before you engage in any formal instruction. Encourage students to wrestle with the problem and come up with some strategies they might use to solve it. Then gather students together and use the guiding questions provided to help them discover key mathematical relationships and understand the special vocabulary used in the problem. This whole-class discussion will enhance student understanding of the problem-solving strategies and math concepts featured in the packet.

The second problem, "Make the Case," uses a multiple-choice format. Three different characters offer possible solutions to the problem. Students have to determine which character—Wally Walrus, Marlee Marlin, Ralph Rhino—has the correct answer. Before they can identify the correct solution, students have to solve the problem themselves and analyze each of the responses. Invite them to speculate about why the other two characters got the wrong answers. (Note: Although we offer a rationale for each wrong answer, other explanations are possible.) As they justify their choices in the "Make the Case" problems, students gain practice and confidence in using math language.

While working on these first two problems, encourage students to talk about their observations and hypotheses. This talk provides a window into what students do and do not understand. Working on "Solve the Problem" and "Make the Case" should take approximately one math period.

The remaining problems in each packet are sequenced by difficulty. They all feature a series of questions that involve analyzing the data display. In the first three or four problems of each set, problem-solving "guru" Ima Thinker provides hints about how to begin solving the problems. The rest of the problems offer no hints. If students have difficulty solving these latter problems, you might want to write "Ima" hints for each of them or ask students to develop hints before beginning to solve the problems. An answer key is provided at the back of the book.

The problem-solving packets are independent of one another and may be used in any order and incorporated into the regular mathematics curriculum at whatever point makes sense. We recommend that you work with each packet in its entirety before moving on to the next one. Once you and your students work through the first two problems, you can assign problems 1 through 7 for students to do on their own or in pairs. You may wish to have them complete the problems during class or for homework.

Using the CD

In addition to the reproducible problem-solving packets in this book, you'll find a CD with ActivInspire (Promethean) files* and PDFs of "Solve the Problem," "Make the Case," and "Solve It" problems, for use on the interactive whiteboard. (Black-line masters of these pages also appear in the book.) Display "Solve the Problem" and "Make the Case" on the whiteboard to help you in leading a whole-class discussion of the problems. Then use the additional "Solve It" problems to guide students in applying our three-step problem-solving process:

1. **Look:** What is the problem? What information do you have? What information do you need?
2. **Plan and Do:** How will you solve the problem? What strategies will you use? What will you do first? What's the next step? What comes after that?
3. **Answer and Check:** What is the answer? How can you be sure that your answer is correct?

These "Solve It" problems encourage writing about mathematics and may be used at any time. They are particularly effective as culminating activities for the problem-solving packets.

*If you do not have ActivInspire software on your computer, click on the folder titled **Promethean Installers**. To install the software on a Mac, double-click on **ActivInspire_v1.6.43277_USA.dmg** file, then click on **ActivInspire.mpkg**. If you have a PC, double-click on **ActivInspireSuite_v1.6.43277_en_US_setup_PC.exe**. Please read the PDF file for the license agreement.

The problem-solving packets in this book support the following Common Core State Standards.

MATHEMATICAL PRACTICES

1. Make sense of problems and persevere in solving them.

2. Reason abstractly and quantitatively.

3. Construct viable arguments and critique the reasoning of others.

4. Model with mathematics.

5. Use appropriate tools strategically.

6. Attend to precision.

7. Look for and make use of structure.

8. Look for and express regularity in repeated reasoning.

OPERATIONS AND ALGEBRAIC THINKING

Use the four operations with whole numbers to solve problems.

4.OA.1 Interpret a multiplication equation as a comparison, e.g., interpret $35 = 5 \times 7$ as a statement that 35 is 5 times as many as 7 and 7 times as many as 5. Represent verbal statements of multiplicative comparisons as multiplication equations.

4.OA.2 Multiply or divide to solve word problems involving multiplicative comparison, e.g., by using drawings and equations with a symbol for the unknown number to represent the problem, distinguishing multiplicative comparison from additive comparison.

4.OA.3 Solve multistep word problems posed with whole numbers and having whole-number answers using the four operations, including problems in which remainders must be interpreted. Represent these problems using equations with a letter standing for the unknown quantity. Assess the reasonableness of answers using mental computation and estimation strategies including rounding.

Gain familiarity with factors and multiples.

4.OA.4 Find all factor pairs for a whole number in the range 1–100. Recognize that a whole number is a multiple of each of its factors. Determine whether a given whole number in the range 1–100 is a multiple of a given one-digit number. Determine whether a given whole number in the range 1–100 is prime or composite.

Generate and analyze patterns.

4.OA.5 Generate a number or shape pattern that follows a given rule. Identify apparent features of the pattern that were not explicit in the rule itself.

References

Common Core State Standards Initiative. (2010). *Common core state standards for mathematics.* Washington, DC: National Governors Association Center for Best Practices and the Council of Chief State School Officers.

Cuevas, Gilbert, & Karol Yeatts. (2001). *Navigating through algebra in grades 3–5.* Reston, VA: National Council of Teachers of Mathematics.

Greenes, Carole, & Carol Findell. (Eds.). (2005). *Developing students' algebraic reasoning abilities.* (Vol. 3 in the NCSM Monograph Series.) Boston, MA: Houghton Mifflin.

Greenes, Carole, & Carol Findell. (2005). *Groundworks: Algebraic thinking.* Chicago: Wright Group/McGraw Hill.

Moses, Barbara (Ed.). (1999). *Algebraic thinking, grades K–12: Readings from NCTM's school-based journals and other publications.* Reston, VA: National Council of Teachers of Mathematics.

National Council of Teachers of Mathematics. (2000). *Principles and standards for school mathematics.* Reston, VA: National Council of Teachers of Mathematics.

Polya, George. (1957). *How to solve it.* Princeton, NJ: Princeton University Press.

Usiskin, Zalman. (1997). Doing algebra in grades K–4. *Teaching Children Mathematics. 3*(6), 346–356.

Dog Data

Overview
Students use clues to interpret mathematical relationships and work backward through the clues to answer questions.

Problem-Solving Strategies
• Work backward
• Use logical reasoning

Related Math Skills
• Compute with whole numbers
• Find fractional parts of groups ($\frac{1}{2}$, $\frac{1}{3}$, $\frac{1}{4}$,)

Algebra Focus
• Represent quantitative relationships with symbols
• Write and solve equations

CCSS Correlation
4.OA.3

Math Language
• Older than
• Younger than
• Twice
• Sum
• One-half
• One-third
• One-fourth

Introducing the Packet
Make photocopies of "Solve the Problem: Dog Data" (page 11) and distribute to students. Have students work in pairs, encouraging them to discuss strategies they might use to solve the problem. You may want to walk around and listen in on some of their discussions. After a few minutes, display the problem on the interactive whiteboard (see the CD) and use the following questions to guide a whole-class discussion on how to solve the problem:

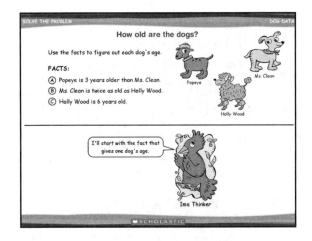

• What did Ima do first to figure out the ages? *(She used Fact C, which gives the only known age. Holly Wood is 6 years old.)*

- Whose age can you figure out next? *(Ms. Clean)*

- Why can't you figure out Popeye's age before figuring out Ms. Clean's age? *(Fact A states that Popeye is 3 years older than Ms. Clean, so we have to figure out Ms. Clean's age before figuring out Popeye's age.)*

- How old is Ms. Clean? *(2 x 6, or 12 years old)*

- How old is Popeye? *(12 + 3, or 15 years old)*

Work together as a class to answer the questions in "Solve the Problem: Dog Data."

Math Chat With "Make the Case"

Display "Make the Case: Dog Data" on the interactive whiteboard. Before students can decide which character is "sharp as a tack," they need to figure out the answer to the problem. Encourage students to work in pairs to solve the problem. Then bring the class together for another whole-class discussion. Ask:

- Who has the right answer? *(Marlee Marlin)*

- How did Marlee Marlin begin to solve the problem? *(She started with Fact C—Windy Day is 4 years old.)*

- What did Marlee Marlin do next? *(She used Fact B—Madam Peppy is 2 years older than Windy Day. Madam Peppy is 4 + 2, or 6 years old.)*

- What did Marlee Marlin do to find Dandy's age? *(She used Fact A and found that Dandy's age is twice Madam Peppy's age. So Dandy is 2 x 6, or 12 years old.)*

- How do you think Wally Walrus got his answer? *(He probably used the numbers in Facts B and C for Madam Peppy and Windy Day's ages and added those two numbers to get Dandy's age.)*

- How do you think Ralph Rhino got his answer? *(He probably found Windy Day's and Madam Peppy's ages the same way that Marlee Marlin did. But then he found Dandy's age by doubling Windy Day's age instead of doubling Madam Peppy's age.)*

Name _____ Date _____

SOLVE THE PROBLEM

How old are the dogs?

Use the facts to figure out each dog's age.

Popeye

Ms. Clean

Holly Wood

FACTS:

(A) Popeye is 3 years older than Ms. Clean.

(B) Ms. Clean is twice as old as Holly Wood.

(C) Holly Wood is 6 years old.

I'll start with the fact that gives one dog's age.

Ima Thinker

1. Which fact did Ima use first? _____

2. How old is Ms. Clean? _____

3. How old is Popeye? _____

4. How did you figure out Popeye's age? _____

_____

Math Problem-Solving Packets: Grade 4 © 2012 by Greenes, Findell & Cavanagh, Scholastic Teaching Resources

Name _____ Date _____

MAKE THE CASE

How old are the dogs?

Use the facts to figure out each dog's age.

Dandy

Madam Peppy

Windy Day

FACTS:

(A) Dandy's age is twice Madam Peppy's age.

(B) Madam Peppy is 2 years older than Windy Day.

(C) Windy Day is 4 years old.

Clearly, Dandy is 6 years old, Madam Peppy is 2 years old, and Windy Day is 4 years old.

Without a doubt, Dandy is 12 years old, Madam Peppy is 6 years old, and Windy Day is 4 years old.

Marlee Marlin

I'm sure that Dandy is 8 years old, Madam Peppy is 6 years old, and Windy Day is 4 years old.

Wally Walrus

Ralph Rhino

12

Who is sharp as a tack?

Math Problem-Solving Packets: Grade 4 © 2012 by Greenes, Findell & Cavanagh, Scholastic Teaching Resources

DOG DATA

How old are the dogs?

Use the facts to figure out each dog's age.

Howdy   **DeVine**   **Bubba**

FACTS:

(A) Howdy is 5 years younger than DeVine.

(B) DeVine's age is half Bubba's age.

(C) Bubba is 14 years old.

> I'll start with the fact that gives one dog's age.

Ima Thinker

1. Which fact did Ima use first? _____

2. How old is DeVine? _____

3. How old is Howdy? _____

4. How did you figure out Howdy's age? _____

_____

Name _____ Date _____

PROBLEM 2

How much do the dogs weigh?

Use the facts to figure out each dog's weight.

Melody

Bubba

Dandy

Windy Day

FACTS:

(A) Melody weighs 4 pounds less than Bubba.

(B) Bubba weighs 10 pounds less than Dandy.

(C) Dandy weighs twice as much as Windy Day.

(D) Windy Day weighs 24 pounds.

I'll start with the fact that gives one dog's weight.

Ima Thinker

1. Which fact did Ima use first? _____

2. How much does Dandy weigh? _____

3. How much does Bubba weigh? _____

4. How did you figure out Melody's weight? _____

_____

Math Problem-Solving Packets: Grade 4 © 2012 by Greenes, Findell & Cavanagh, Scholastic Teaching Resources

Name _____ Date _____

PROBLEM 3

How much do the dogs weigh?

Use the facts to figure out each dog's weight.

Spot   Popeye   DeVine   Madam Peppy

FACTS:

(A) Spot weighs 4 pounds less than DeVine.

(B) Popeye weighs half as much as DeVine.

(C) DeVine's weight is ten times Madam Peppy's weight.

(D) Madam Peppy weighs 5 pounds.

I'll start with the fact that gives one dog's weight.

Ima Thinker

1. Which fact did Ima use first? _____

2. How much does DeVine weigh? _____ ____

3. How much does Popeye weigh? _____

4. How did you figure out Spot's weight? _____

_____

Name _____ Date _____

How much do the dogs weigh?

Use the facts to figure out each dog's weight.

Betsy   Howdy   Holly Wood   Ms. Clean

FACTS:

(A) Betsy weighs 10 pounds less than Howdy.

(B) Howdy's weight is 17 pounds more than Holly Wood's weight.

(C) Holly Wood's weight is twice Ms. Clean's weight.

(D) Ms. Clean weighs 19 pounds.

1. Which fact did you use first? _____

2. How much does Holly Wood weigh? _____

3. How much does Howdy weigh? _____

4. How did you figure out Betsy's weight? _____

_____

Math Problem-Solving Packets: Grade 4 © 2012 by Greenes, Findell & Cavanagh, Scholastic Teaching Resources

Name _____ Date _____

PROBLEM 5

How many ounces of dog food does each dog eat in one day?

Use the facts to figure out how much food each dog eats.

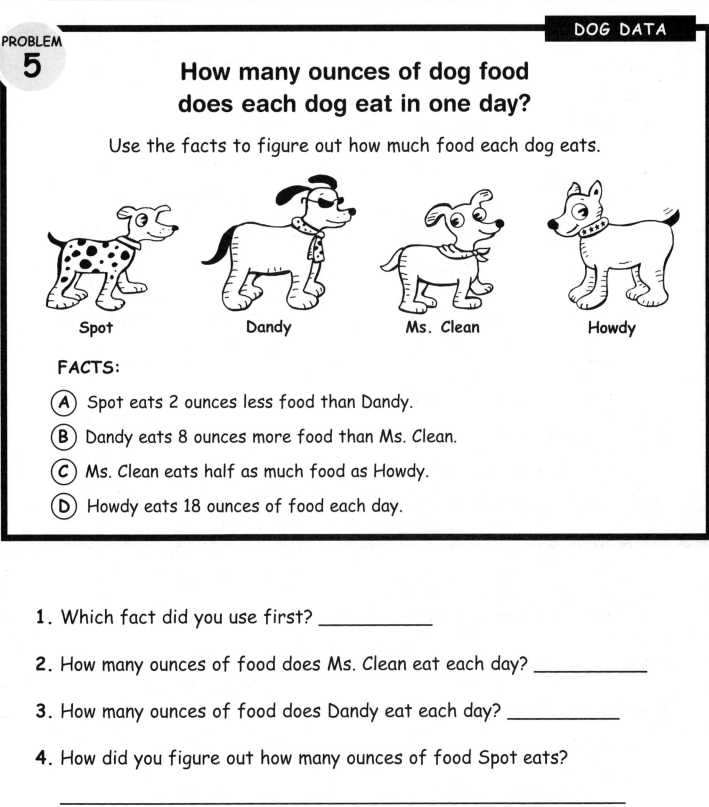

Spot   Dandy   Ms. Clean   Howdy

FACTS:

(A) Spot eats 2 ounces less food than Dandy.

(B) Dandy eats 8 ounces more food than Ms. Clean.

(C) Ms. Clean eats half as much food as Howdy.

(D) Howdy eats 18 ounces of food each day.

1. Which fact did you use first? _____

2. How many ounces of food does Ms. Clean eat each day? _____

3. How many ounces of food does Dandy eat each day? _____

4. How did you figure out how many ounces of food Spot eats?

_____

_____

Name _____   Date _____

PROBLEM 6

How many ounces of dog food does each dog eat in one day?

Use the facts to figure out how much food each dog eats.

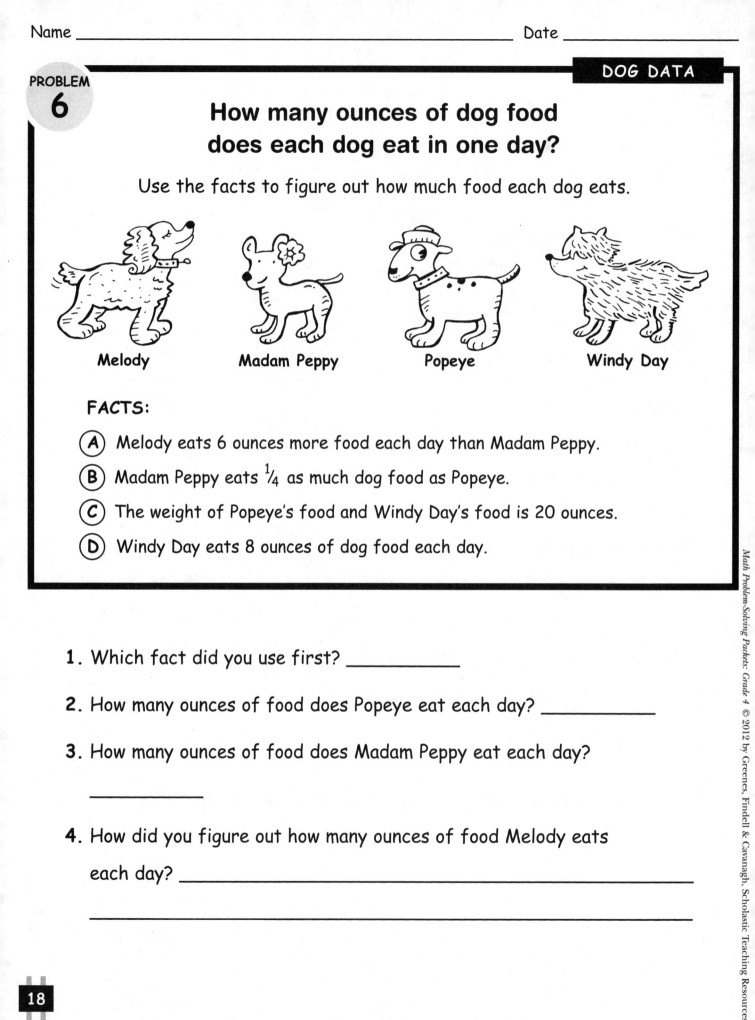

Melody   Madam Peppy   Popeye   Windy Day

FACTS:

Ⓐ Melody eats 6 ounces more food each day than Madam Peppy.

Ⓑ Madam Peppy eats $\frac{1}{4}$ as much dog food as Popeye.

Ⓒ The weight of Popeye's food and Windy Day's food is 20 ounces.

Ⓓ Windy Day eats 8 ounces of dog food each day.

1. Which fact did you use first? _____

2. How many ounces of food does Popeye eat each day? _____

3. How many ounces of food does Madam Peppy eat each day?

   _____

4. How did you figure out how many ounces of food Melody eats

   each day? _____

   _____

Math Problem-Solving Packets: Grade 4 © 2012 by Greenes, Findell & Cavanagh, Scholastic Teaching Resources

Math Problem-Solving Packets: Grade 4 · © 2012 by Greenes, Findell & Cavanagh, Scholastic Teaching Resources

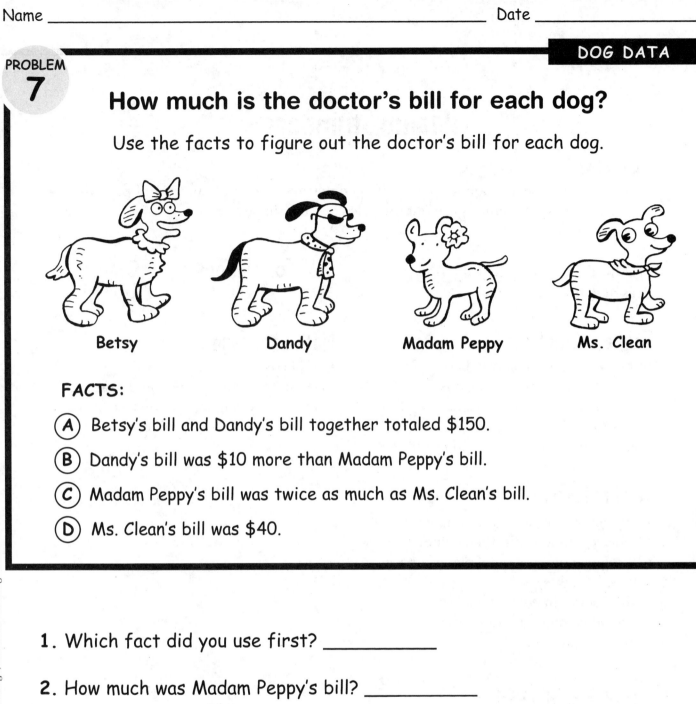

DOG DATA

PROBLEM 7

How much is the doctor's bill for each dog?

Use the facts to figure out the doctor's bill for each dog.

Betsy   Dandy   Madam Peppy   Ms. Clean

FACTS:

(A) Betsy's bill and Dandy's bill together totaled $150.

(B) Dandy's bill was $10 more than Madam Peppy's bill.

(C) Madam Peppy's bill was twice as much as Ms. Clean's bill.

(D) Ms. Clean's bill was $40.

1. Which fact did you use first? _____

2. How much was Madam Peppy's bill? _____

3. How much was Dandy's bill? _____

4. How did you figure out how much Betsy's bill was? _____

_____

Stamp Stumpers

Overview
Presented with a set of stamps—some with geometric shapes and others with prices—and its total cost, students figure out the price of each shape stamp.

Problem-Solving Strategy
Reason deductively

Related Math Skills
• Compute with whole numbers
• Recognize chevrons, hexagons, octagons, pentagons, squares, trapezoids, and triangles
• Recognize cones, cubes, and cylinders

Algebra Focus
• Solve equations with one variable
• Replace symbols with their values
• Recognize that the same pictures have the same value
• Understand that taking away an addend changes the sum by the same amount

CCSS Correlations
4.OA.2 • 4.OA.3

Math Language
• Total cost
• Geometric shapes: chevron, hexagon, octagon, pentagon, square, trapezoid, triangle, cone, cube, cylinder

Introducing the Packet
Make photocopies of "Solve the Problem: Stamp Stumpers" (page 22) and distribute to students. Have students work in pairs, encouraging them to discuss strategies they might use to solve the problem. You may want to walk around and listen in on some of their discussions. After a few minutes, display the problem on the interactive whiteboard (see the CD) and use the following questions to guide a whole-class discussion on how to solve the problem:

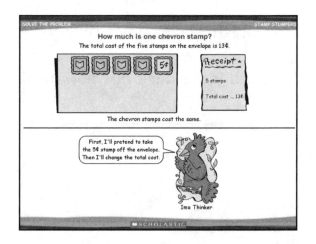

- What do you see? *(4 chevron stamps, one 5¢ stamp, and a receipt showing a total cost of 13¢)*

- What do you need to figure out in this problem? *(The cost of one chevron stamp)*

- What will you do first? *(Take away the 5¢ stamp and change the total cost.)*

- What is the new cost? *(13¢ − 5¢, or 8¢)*

- What does this new sum represent? *(The cost of the 4 chevron stamps)*

- How can you figure out the cost of each chevron stamp? *(If 4 chevron stamps are 8¢, then one chevron is 8¢ ÷ 4, or 2¢.)*

Work together as a class to answer the questions in "Solve the Problem: Stamp Stumpers."

Math Chat With "Make the Case"

Display "Make the Case: Stamp Stumpers" on the interactive whiteboard. Before students can decide which character is "sharp as a tack," they need to figure out the answer to the problem. Encourage students to work in pairs to solve the problem. Then bring the class together for another whole-class discussion. Ask:

- Who has the right answer? *(Ralph Rhino)*

- How did you figure it out?
  (21¢ − 3¢ − 6¢ = 12¢; and 12¢ ÷ 3 = 4¢)

- How do you think Wally Walrus got the answer 5¢? *(He probably subtracted the 6¢ from 21¢ and got 15¢. 15¢ ÷ 3 = 5¢. He forgot to subtract both the 6¢ and the 3¢ from 21¢.)*

- How do you think Marlee Marlin got the answer 6¢? *(She probably subtracted the 3¢ from 21¢ and got 18¢, then 18¢ ÷ 3 = 6¢. She forgot to subtract both the 3¢ and the 6¢ from 21¢.)*

Name _____ Date _____

SOLVE THE PROBLEM

How much is one chevron stamp?

The total cost of the five stamps on the envelope is 13¢.

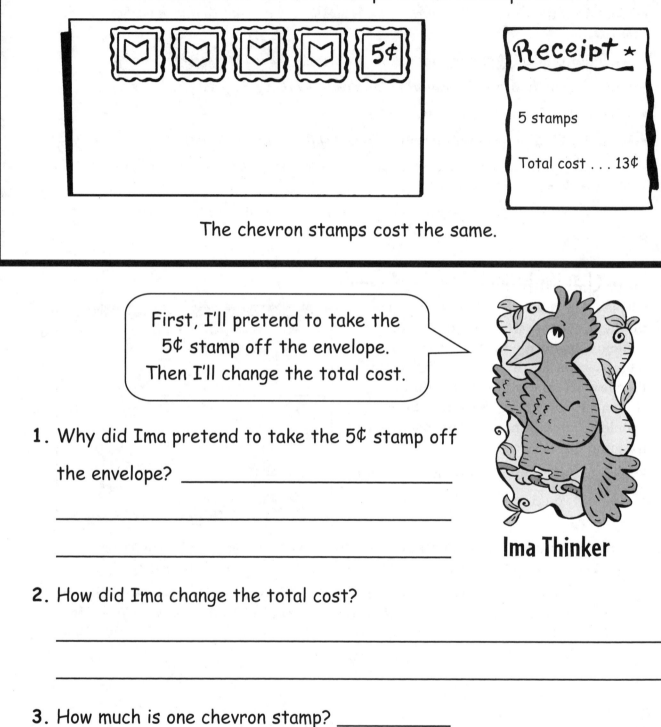

Receipt *

5 stamps

Total cost . . . 13¢

The chevron stamps cost the same.

First, I'll pretend to take the 5¢ stamp off the envelope. Then I'll change the total cost.

Ima Thinker

1. Why did Ima pretend to take the 5¢ stamp off the envelope? _____

_____

_____

2. How did Ima change the total cost?

_____

_____

3. How much is one chevron stamp? _____

4. How did you figure out the answer to #3? _____

_____

Math Problem-Solving Packets: Grade 4 © 2012 by Greenes, Findell & Cavanagh, Scholastic Teaching Resources

MAKE THE CASE

How much is one trapezoid stamp?

The total cost of the five stamps on the envelope is 21¢.

3¢ 6¢

Receipt ★

5 stamps

Total cost . . . 21¢

The trapezoid stamps cost the same.

That's easy. One trapezoid stamp costs 5¢.

I'm sure it costs 6¢.

Marlee Marlin

You're both wrong. It has to be 4¢.

Wally Walrus

Ralph Rhino

Who is sharp as a tack?

Name _____ Date _____

PROBLEM 1

How much is one octagon stamp?

The total cost of the four stamps on the envelope is 17¢.

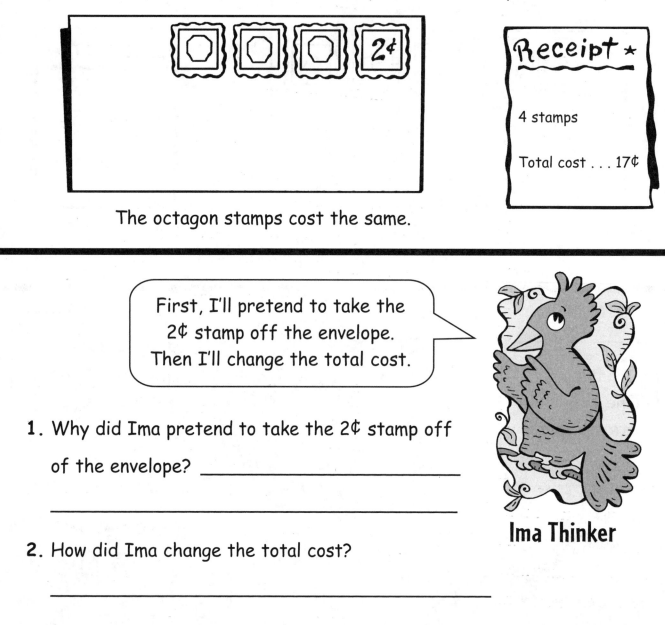

The octagon stamps cost the same.

First, I'll pretend to take the 2¢ stamp off the envelope. Then I'll change the total cost.

Ima Thinker

1. Why did Ima pretend to take the 2¢ stamp off of the envelope? _____
_____

2. How did Ima change the total cost?

_____

_____

3. How much is one octagon stamp? _____

4. How did you figure out the answer to #3?

_____

_____

Math Problem-Solving Packets: Grade 4 © 2012 by Greenes, Findell & Cavanagh, Scholastic Teaching Resources

PROBLEM 2

How much is one pentagon stamp?

The total cost of the four stamps on the envelope is 33¢.

3¢

Receipt ⋆

4 stamps

Total cost . . . 33¢

The pentagon stamps cost the same.

> First, I'll pretend to take the 3¢ stamp off the envelope. Then, I'll change the total cost.

Ima Thinker

1. How did Ima change the total cost?

_____

_____

2. How much is one pentagon stamp? _____

3. How did you figure out the answer to #2?

_____

_____

4. Write the cost on each pentagon stamp below. Find the total cost.

2¢ 8¢

Receipt ⋆

4 stamps

Total cost . . . ____¢

PROBLEM 3

How much is one triangle stamp?

The total cost of the four stamps on the envelope is 29¢.

△ △ △ 8¢

Receipt ★

4 stamps

Total cost . . . 29¢

The triangle stamps cost the same.

First, I'll pretend to take the 8¢ stamp off the envelope. Then, I'll change the total cost.

Ima Thinker

1. How did Ima change the total cost?

_____

_____

2. How much is one triangle stamp? _____

3. How did you figure out the answer to #2?

_____

4. Write the cost on each triangle stamp below. Find the total cost.

△ △ △ △ 2¢

Receipt ★

5 stamps

Total cost . . . ____ ¢

Math Problem-Solving Packets: Grade 4 © 2012 by Greenes, Findell & Cavanagh, Scholastic Teaching Resources

Name _____   Date _____

PROBLEM 4

How much is one square stamp?

The total cost of the five stamps on the envelope is 25¢.

☐ ☐ ☐ ☐ **1¢**

Receipt ★

5 stamps

Total cost . . . 25¢

The square stamps cost the same.

1. How much is each square stamp? _____

2. How did you figure out the answer to #1? _____

_____

3. Write the cost on each square stamp below. What is the total cost?

_____

☐ ☐ ☐ **2¢**

Receipt ★

4 stamps

Total cost . . . ____¢

4. Write the cost on each square stamp below. What is the missing number?

_____

☐ ☐ __¢

Receipt ★

3 stamps

Total cost . . . 20¢

PROBLEM 5

How much is one cylinder stamp?

The total cost of the five stamps on the envelope is 15¢.

Receipt ★

5 stamps

Total cost . . . 15¢

The cylinder stamps cost the same.

1. How much is each cylinder stamp? _____

2. How did you figure out the answer to #1? _____

_____

3. Write the cost on each cylinder stamp below. What is the total cost?

_____

Receipt ★

3 stamps

Total cost . . . ____¢

4. Write the cost on each cylinder stamp below. What is the cost of the

fourth stamp? _____

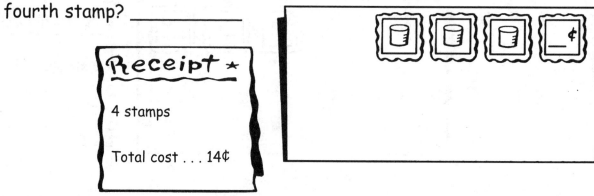

Receipt ★

4 stamps

Total cost . . . 14¢

Math Problem-Solving Packets: Grade 4 © 2012 by Greenes, Findell & Cavanagh, Scholastic Teaching Resources

Name _____ Date _____

PROBLEM 6

How much is one cube stamp?

The total cost of the five stamps on the envelope is 31¢.

| □ | □ | □ | 5¢ | 2¢ |

Receipt ★

5 stamps

Total cost . . . 31¢

The cube stamps cost the same.

1. How much is one cube stamp? _____

2. How did you figure out the answer to #1? _____

_____

3. Write the cost on each cube stamp below. What is the total cost?

_____

| □ | □ | □ | 4¢ |

Receipt ★

4 stamps

Total cost . . . ____¢

4. Write the cost on each cube stamp. What is the cost of the fourth

stamp?

_____

| □ | □ | 3¢ | __¢ |

Receipt ★

4 stamps

Total cost . . . 28¢

PROBLEM 7

How much is one hexagon stamp?

The total cost of the five stamps on the envelope is 40¢.

Receipt ★

5 stamps

Total cost . . . 40¢

The hexagon stamps cost the same.

1. How much is each hexagon stamp? _____

2. How did you figure out the answer to #1? _____

_____

3. Write the cost in each hexagon below. What is the total cost?

_____

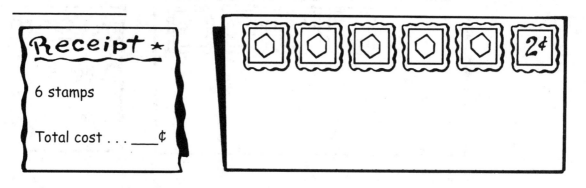

Receipt ★

6 stamps

Total cost . . . ___¢

4. Write the cost in each hexagon. What is the missing number?

_____

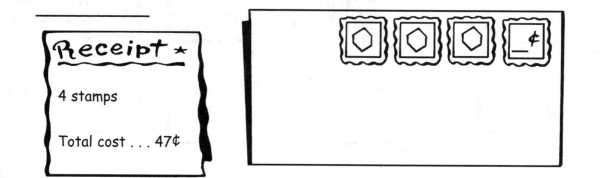

Receipt ★

4 stamps

Total cost . . . 47¢

Math Problem-Solving Packets: Grade 4 © 2012 by Greenes, Findell & Cavanagh, Scholastic Teaching Resources

Jersey Number

Overview
Students use clues and reason logically to figure out the number represented by a letter on a player's jersey.

Problem-Solving Strategies
- Make a list of possible solutions
- Test possible solutions with clues
- Use logical reasoning

Related Math Skills
- Compute with whole numbers
- Compare numbers
- Identify factors of numbers
- Identify odd and even numbers

Algebra Focus
- Solve for values of unknowns
- Replace letters with their values

CCSS Correlations
4.OA.3 • 4.OA.4

Math Language
- Less than <
- Greater than >
- Digit
- Difference
- Sum
- Even number
- Odd number
- Factor

Introducing the Packet
Make photocopies of "Solve the Problem: Jersey Number" (page 33) and distribute to students. Have students work in pairs, encouraging them to discuss strategies they might use to solve the problem. You may want to walk around and listen in on some of their discussions. After a few minutes, display the problem on the interactive whiteboard (see the CD) and use the following questions to guide a whole-class discussion on how to solve the problem:

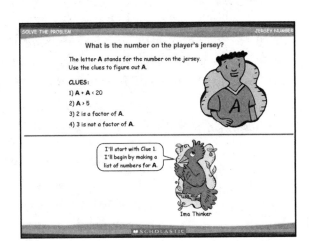

- Why is 9 the greatest number on Ima's list? *(Clue 1 shows that when A is added to itself, the sum is less than 20. Since A must be less than 10, then the greatest number that A can represent is 9; 9 + 9 = 18.)*

- What other numbers are on Ima's list? *(8, 7, 6, 5, 4, 3, 2, 1, and 0)*

- Which clue do you think Ima will use next? *(Any of the clues will give useful information. If Ima uses Clue 2, she can cross off 0, 1, 2, 3, 4, and 5. That leaves 6, 7, 8, and 9.)*

- What does Clue 3 mean? *(A is an even number. When you divide A by 2, you get a whole number for an answer.)*

- Which numbers does Clue 3 eliminate? *(7 and 9)*

- Which remaining number fits Clue 4? *(8)*

Work together as a class to answer the questions in "Solve the Problem: Jersey Number."

Math Chat With "Make the Case"

Display "Make the Case: Jersey Number" on the interactive whiteboard. Before students can decide which character is "sharp as a tack," they need to figure out the answer to the problem. Encourage students to work in pairs to solve the problem. Then bring the class together for another whole-class discussion. Ask:

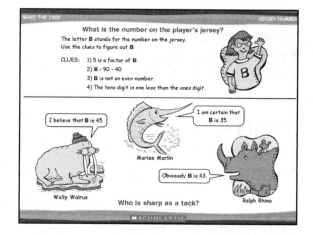

- Who has the right answer? *(Wally Walrus)*

- How did you figure it out? *(From Clue 2, B is less than 90 – 40, or 50. So B can be 49 or less. Make a list of those numbers. From Clue 1, B has to have a factor of 5, so eliminate all numbers except for 5, 10, 15, 20, 25, 30, 35, 40, and 45. Clue 3 eliminates all even numbers leaving 5, 15, 25, 35, and 45. Clue 4 indicates that the tens digit is one less than the ones digit. Only 45 fits that clue.)*

- How do you think Marlee Marlin got the answer 35? *(35 fits clues 1, 2, and 3. Marlee Marlin probably forgot to use Clue 4.)*

- How do you think Ralph Rhino got the answer 43? *(43 fits clues 2, 3, and 4. Ralph Rhino probably forgot to use Clue 1.)*

Math Problem-Solving Packets: Grade 4 © 2012 by Greenes, Findell & Cavanagh, Scholastic Teaching Resources

Name _____ Date _____

SOLVE THE PROBLEM

What is the number on the player's jersey?

The letter **A** stands for the number on the jersey.

Use the clues to figure out **A**.

CLUES:
1) **A** + **A** < 20
2) **A** > 5
3) 2 is a factor of **A**
4) 3 is not a factor of **A**

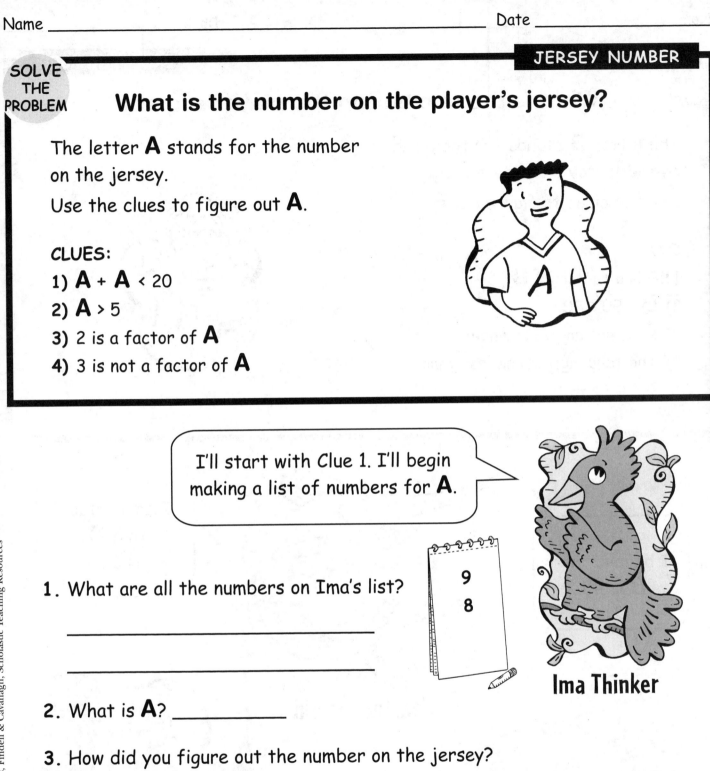

I'll start with Clue 1. I'll begin making a list of numbers for **A**.

Ima Thinker

9
8

1. What are all the numbers on Ima's list?

   _____

   _____

2. What is **A**? _____

3. How did you figure out the number on the jersey?

   _____

   _____

4. Check your number with the clues. Show your work here.

MAKE THE CASE

What is the number on the player's jersey?

The letter **B** stands for the number on the jersey.

Use the clues to figure out **B**.

CLUES:

1) 5 is a factor of **B**
2) **B** < 90 – 40
3) **B** is not an even number
4) The tens digit is one less than the ones digit

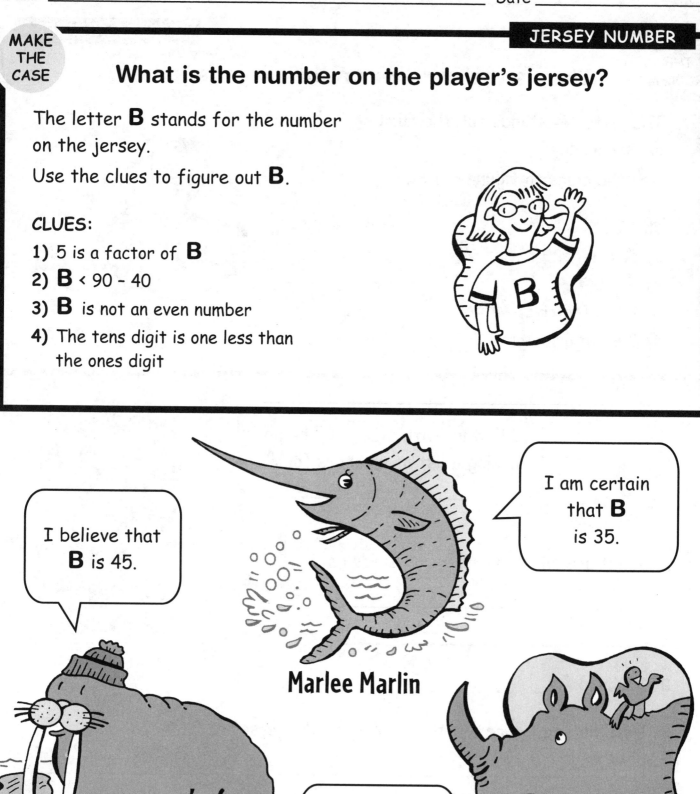

I believe that **B** is 45.

Wally Walrus

Marlee Marlin

I am certain that **B** is 35.

Obviously **B** is 43.

Ralph Rhino

Who is sharp as a tack?

Math Problem-Solving Packets: Grade 4 © 2012 by Greenes, Findell & Cavanagh, Scholastic Teaching Resources

PROBLEM 1

What is the number on the player's jersey?

The letter **C** stands for the number on the jersey.
Use the clues to figure out **C**.

CLUES:

1) $C < 6 + 10$
2) **C** is an odd number
3) 5 is not a factor of **C**
4) 3 is a factor of **C**
5) **C** is not 3×3

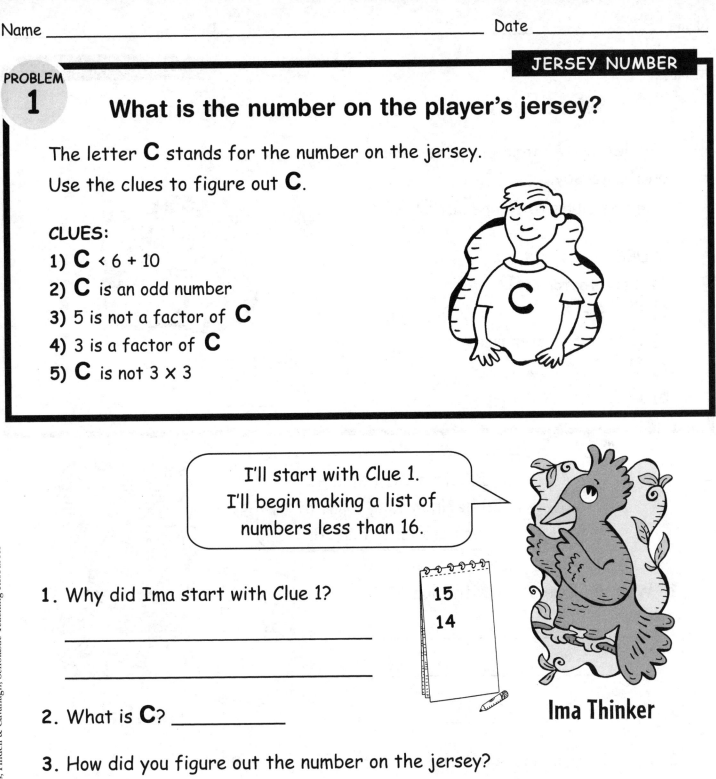

I'll start with Clue 1.
I'll begin making a list of
numbers less than 16.

15
14

Ima Thinker

1. Why did Ima start with Clue 1?

_____

_____

2. What is **C**? _____

3. How did you figure out the number on the jersey?

_____

_____

4. Check your number with the clues. Show your work here.

PROBLEM 2

What is the number on the player's jersey?

The letter **D** stands for the number on the jersey.

Use the clues to figure out **D**.

CLUES:

1) 3 is a factor of **D**

2) **D** > 9 – 4

3) **D** is not an even number

4) **D** < 18

5) **D** is not 2 × 2 + 5

I'll start with Clue 4. I'll begin making a list of numbers less than 18.

1. Why did Ima start with Clue 4?

   _____

   _____

17
16

Ima Thinker

2. What is **D**? _____

3. How did you figure out the number on the jersey?

   _____

   _____

4. Check your number with the clues. Show your work here.

Math Problem-Solving Packets: Grade 4 © 2012 by Greenes, Findell & Cavanagh, Scholastic Teaching Resources

PROBLEM 3

What is the number on the player's jersey?

The letter **E** stands for the number on the jersey.

Use the clues to figure out **E**.

CLUES:
1) **E** > 10 − 8
2) **E** is not an even number
3) **E** + **E** + **E** < 24
4) 3 is not a factor of **E**
5) **E** is not 1 × 5

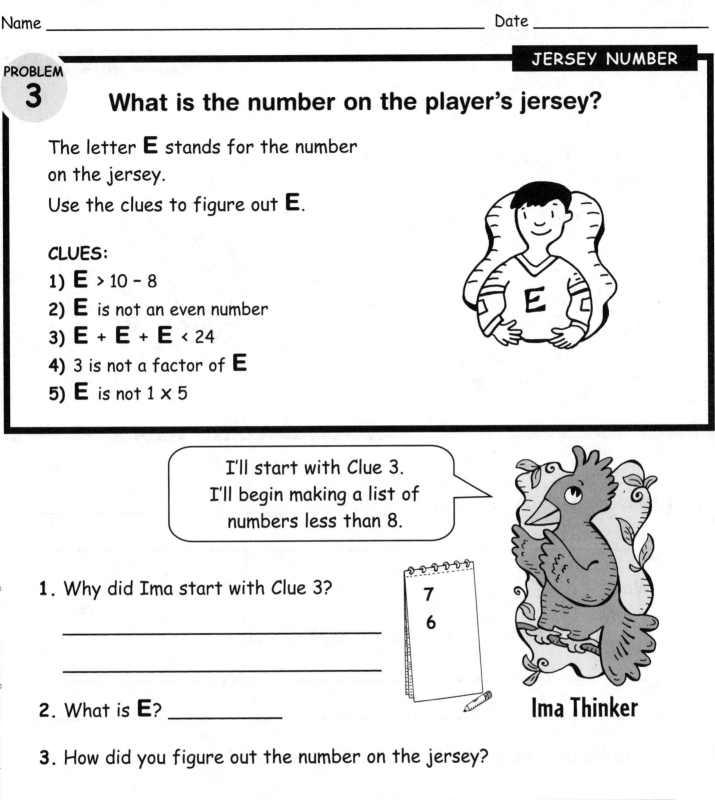

I'll start with Clue 3.
I'll begin making a list of numbers less than 8.

1. Why did Ima start with Clue 3?

_____

_____

2. What is **E**? _____

3. How did you figure out the number on the jersey?

_____

_____

4. Check your number with the clues. Show your work here.

7
6

Ima Thinker

Math Problem-Solving Packets: Grade 4 © 2012 by Greenes, Findell & Cavanagh, Scholastic Teaching Resources

PROBLEM
4

What is the number on the player's jersey?

The letter **F** stands for the number on the jersey.

Use the clues to figure out **F**.

CLUES:
1) **F** + **F** < 20
2) **F** + **F** + **F** > 12
3) **F** is not an odd number
4) 3 is not a factor of **F**

1. Which clue did you use first? Why? _____

_____

2. What is **F**? _____

3. How did you figure out the number on the jersey?

_____

_____

4. Check your number with the clues. Show your work here.

Math Problem-Solving Teaching Packets: Grade 4 © 2012 by Greenes, Findell & Cavanagh, Scholastic Teaching Resources

PROBLEM 5

What is the number on the player's jersey?

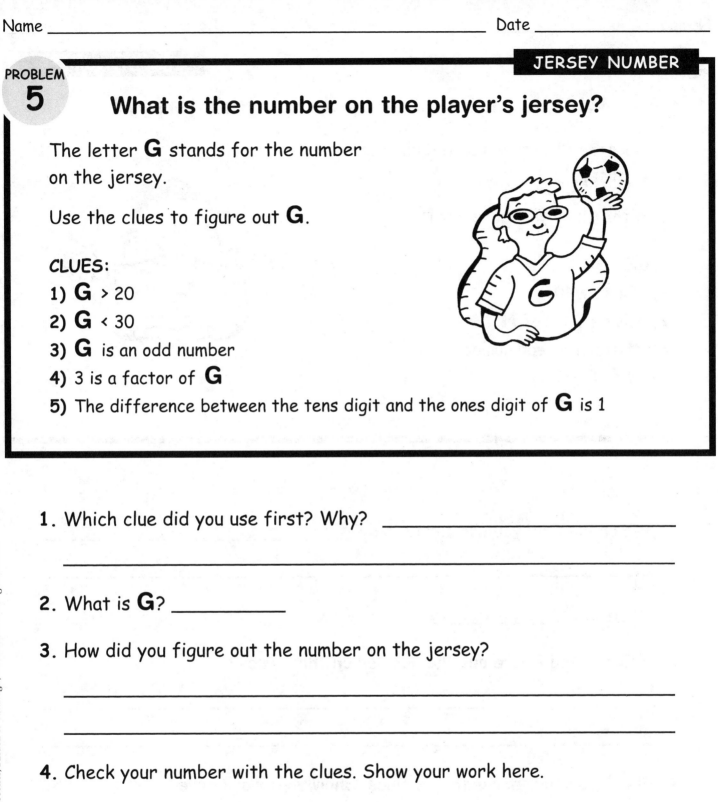

The letter **G** stands for the number on the jersey.

Use the clues to figure out **G**.

CLUES:

1) **G** > 20

2) **G** < 30

3) **G** is an odd number

4) 3 is a factor of **G**

5) The difference between the tens digit and the ones digit of **G** is 1

1. Which clue did you use first? Why? _____

_____

2. What is **G**? _____

3. How did you figure out the number on the jersey?

_____

_____

4. Check your number with the clues. Show your work here.

PROBLEM 6

What is the number on the player's jersey?

The letter **H** stands for the number on the jersey.

Use the clues to figure out **H**.

CLUES:
1) $4 \times$ **H** > 40
2) 3 is a factor of **H**
3) **H** is not an odd number
4) **H** $< 40 \div 2$
5) The sum of the digits of **H** is not 9

1. Which clue did you use first? Why? _____

_____

2. What is **H**? _____

3. How did you figure out the number on the jersey?

_____

_____

4. Check your number with the clues. Show your work here.

Math Problem-Solving Packets: Grade 4 © 2012 by Greenes, Findell & Cavanagh, Scholastic Teaching Resources

PROBLEM 7

What is the number on the player's jersey?

The letter **J** stands for the number on the jersey.

Use the clues to figure out **J**.

CLUES:

1) **J** > 20
2) **J** < 10 + 30
3) The ones digit of **J** is greater than the tens digit
4) 5 is a factor of **J**
5) The sum of the digits of **J** is an even number

1. Which clue did you use first? Why? _____

    _____

2. What is **J**? _____

3. How did you figure out the number on the jersey?

    _____

    _____

4. Check your number with the clues. Show your work here.

Weigh In

Overview

Students examine three scales, each showing the total weight of kids, animals, and other objects, then solve for the weight of each.

Problem-Solving Strategies

- Reason deductively
- Test cases

Related Math Skill

Compute with whole numbers

Algebra Focus

- Solve two or three equations with two or three unknowns
- Replace unknowns with their values

CCSS Correlations

4.OA.2 • 4.OA.3

Math Language

- Pounds
- Scale
- Weigh
- Total weight

Introducing the Packet

Make photocopies of "Solve the Problem: Weigh In" (page 44) and distribute to students. Have students work in pairs, encouraging them to discuss strategies they might use to solve the problem. You may want to walk around and listen in on some of their discussions. After a few minutes, display the problem on the interactive whiteboard (see the CD) and use the following questions to guide a whole-class discussion on how to solve the problem:

- Look at the three scales. Who are on scale A? *(Tom and Smudge the cat)*

- Who is on scale B? *(Tom)*

- Who are on scale C? *(Tom and Alex the dog)*

- Whose weight do you know for sure? *(Tom's weight)* How do you know? *(He is the only one on scale B.)*

- How can knowing that Tom weighs 85 pounds help you figure out Smudge's weight? *(If Tom weighs 85 pounds, and the total weight of Tom and Smudge is 100 pounds, then Smudge must weigh 100 – 85, or 15 pounds.)*

- How can you figure out Alex's weight? *(On scale C, Tom and Alex weigh a total of 125 pounds. Since Tom weighs 85 pounds, Alex weighs 125 – 85, or 40 pounds.)*

Work together as a class to answer the questions in "Solve the Problem: Weigh In."

Math Chat With "Make the Case"

Display "Make the Case: Weigh In" on the interactive whiteboard. Before students can decide which character is "sharp as a tack," they need to figure out the answer to the problem. Encourage students to work in pairs to solve the problem. Then bring the class together for another whole-class discussion. Ask:

- Who has the right answer? *(Ralph Rhino)*

- How did you figure it out? *(On scale C, five bags of rocks weighed 10 pounds. So one bag of rocks is 10 ÷ 5, or 2 pounds. Since a bag of rocks is 2 pounds, the fishbowl on scale B is 7 – 2, or 5 pounds. Since a fishbowl weighs 5 pounds, James on scale A must weigh 75 – 5, or 70 pounds.)*

- How do you think Wally Walrus got the answer of 68 pounds? *(He probably subtracted the weights of both the bag of rocks and the fishbowl, or 7 pounds, from 75 pounds.)*

- How do you think Marlee Marlin got the answer of 73? *(She probably subtracted the weight of the bag of rocks from 75 pounds instead of subtracting the weight of one fishbowl.)*

SOLVE THE PROBLEM

How much does each one weigh?

Scale A   Scale B   Scale C

I know how much Tom weighs. I'll write that number on all his pictures.

Ima Thinker

1. What number of pounds will Ima write

   on Tom's pictures? _____

2. Alex the dog weighs _____ pounds.

3. Smudge the cat weighs _____ pounds.

4. How did you figure out the number of pounds for Smudge?

   _____

   _____

44

MAKE THE CASE

How much does James weigh?

Who is sharp as a tack?

45

Name _____ Date _____

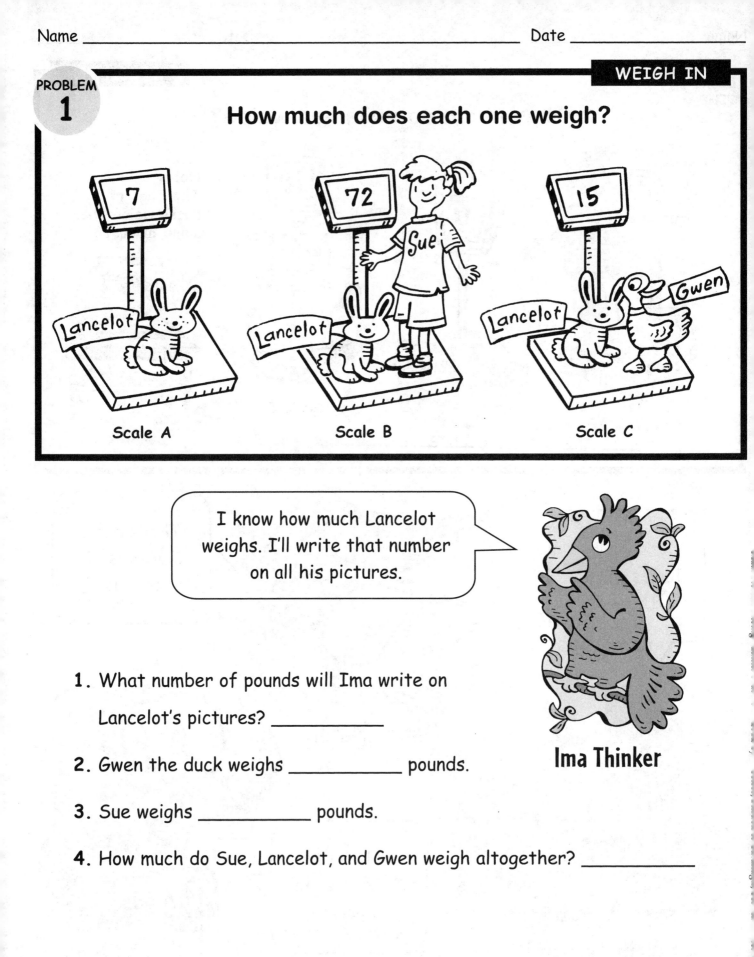

PROBLEM 1

WEIGH IN

How much does each one weigh?

Scale A   Scale B   Scale C

I know how much Lancelot weighs. I'll write that number on all his pictures.

Ima Thinker

1. What number of pounds will Ima write on

   Lancelot's pictures? _____

2. Gwen the duck weighs _____ pounds.

3. Sue weighs _____ pounds.

4. How much do Sue, Lancelot, and Gwen weigh altogether? _____

46

Name _____ Date _____

PROBLEM 2

WEIGH IN

How much does each one weigh?

Scale A   Scale B   Scale C

I know how much Daniel weighs. I'll write that number on all his pictures.

Ima Thinker

1. What number of pounds will Ima write on

   the pictures of Daniel? _____

2. Lisa weighs _____ pounds.

3. Sly the snake weighs _____ pounds.

4. How much more does Daniel weigh than Lisa? _____

How much does each one weigh?

Scale A Scale B Scale C

I know how much Jenna weighs. I'll write that number on all her pictures.

Ima Thinker

1. What number of pounds will Ima write on the pictures of Jenna? _____

2. Keisha weighs _____ pounds.

3. Sasha the dog weighs _____ pounds.

4. Altogether, Jenna, Keisha, and Sasha weigh _____ pounds.

Name _____ Date _____

How much does each one weigh?

Scale A   Scale B   Scale C

1. Billy the goat weighs _____ pounds.

2. Nancy weighs _____ pounds.

3. Horace the rabbit weighs _____ pounds.

4. How much more does Billy weigh than Horace? _____

PROBLEM
5

How much does each one weigh?

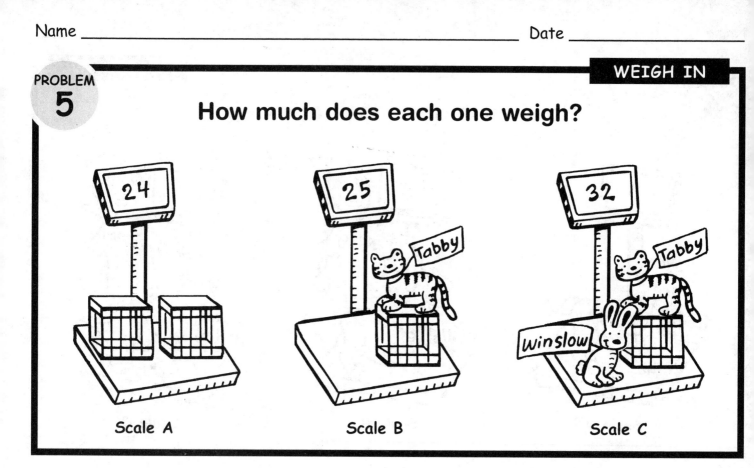

Scale A   Scale B   Scale C

1. One cage weighs _____ pounds.

2. Tabby the cat weighs _____ pounds.

3. Winslow the rabbit weighs _____ pounds.

4. How did you figure out how much Winslow weighs?

_____

_____

Math Problem-Solving Packets: Grade 4 © 2012 by Greenes, Findell & Cavanagh, Scholastic Teaching Resources

Name _____ Date _____

PROBLEM
6

How much does each one weigh?

Scale A   Scale B   Scale C

1. One bag of dog food weighs _____ pounds.

2. Bowser the dog weighs _____ pounds.

3. Mario weighs _____ pounds.

4. How did you figure out how much Mario weighs?

_____

_____

PROBLEM 7

How much does each one weigh?

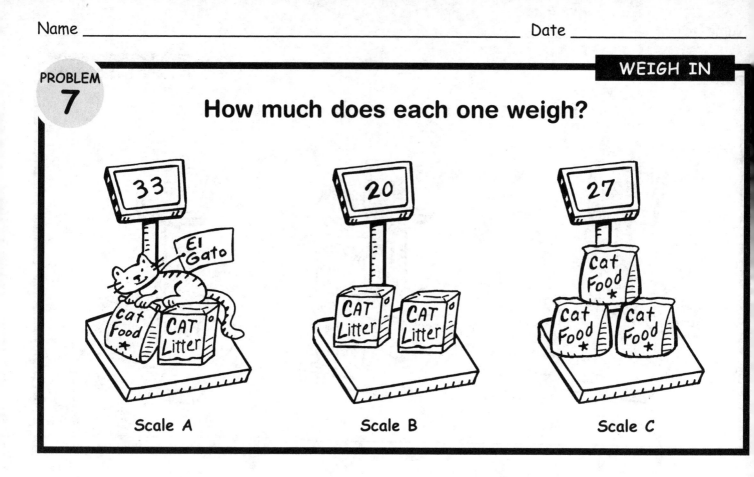

Scale A   Scale B   Scale C

1. One box of cat litter weighs _____ pounds.

2. One bag of cat food weighs _____ pounds.

3. El Gato the cat weighs _____ pounds.

4. How did you figure out how much El Gato weighs?

_____

_____

Balancing Animals

Overview
Shown two pan balances with toy animals, students identify how many of one type of toy animal will balance another type of toy animal.

Problem-Solving Strategy
Reason about proportional relationships

Related Math Skill
Compute with whole numbers

Algebra Focus
- Understand that substituting one set of animals with a second set of equal weight preserves balance
- Explore equality through the use of pan balances

CCSS Correlations
4.OA.2 • 4.OA.3 • 4.OA.4

Math Language
- Balance
- Weigh the same

Introducing the Packet
Make photocopies of "Solve the Problem: Balancing Animals" (page 55) and distribute to students. Have students work in pairs, encouraging them to discuss strategies they might use to solve the problem. You may want to walk around and listen in on some of their discussions. After a few minutes, display the problem on the interactive whiteboard (see the CD) and use the following questions to guide a whole-class discussion on how to solve the problem:

- Look at the pan balances. What do you see? (*Two pan balances that show equal weights. The first pan balance shows that 2 fish balance one frog. The second pan balance shows that 3 frogs balance one shark.*)

- Which weighs more—one frog or one fish? *(One frog)* How do you know? *(It takes 2 fish to balance one frog, so the frog weighs twice as much as one fish, or one fish is half the weight of one frog.)*

- What do you need to figure out? *(How many fish will balance one shark?)*

- What will you do first? *(Write "2 fish" on each frog in the second pan balance.)*

- If one frog weighs 2 pounds, how many pounds is one shark? *(6 pounds)* How do you know? *(3 frogs balance one shark, and 2 + 2 + 2 = 6)*

Work together as a class to answer the questions in "Solve the Problem: Balancing Animals."

Math Chat With "Make the Case"

Display "Make the Case: Balancing Animals" on the interactive whiteboard. Before students can decide which character is "sharp as a tack," they need to figure out the answer to the problem. Encourage students to work in pairs to solve the problem. Then bring the class together for another whole-class discussion. Ask:

- Who has the right answer? *(Wally Walrus)*

- How did you figure it out?
  (One crab balances 3 clams, so 2 crabs will balance 6 clams. Since 6 clams balance 1 lobster, 2 crabs balance 1 lobster.)

- How do you think Marlee Marlin got the answer 3? *(She probably mixed up crabs and clams, and forgot to multiply the 3 clams by 2.)*

- How do you think Ralph Rhino got the answer 18? *(He probably multiplied 3 times the number of clams in the second pan: 3 x 6 = 18.)*

SOLVE THE PROBLEM

How many fish will balance one shark?

Toy animals that are the same weigh the same.

I know how many fish balance one frog. I'll write that number of fish on each frog.

Ima Thinker

1. What number of fish will Ima write

   on each frog? _____

2. How many frogs balance one shark? _____

3. How many fish will balance one shark? _____

4. How did you figure out the answer to #3? _____

   _____

55

MAKE THE CASE

How many crabs will balance one lobster?

Toy animals that are the same weigh the same.

That's easy. Two crabs will balance one lobster.

Obviously it's 3 crabs.

Marlee Marlin

You're both wrong. I am sure it's 18 crabs.

Wally Walrus

Ralph Rhino

Who is sharp as a tack?

Name _____ Date _____

PROBLEM 1

How many cats will balance one cow?

Toy animals that are the same weigh the same.

I know how many cats balance two pigs. I'll write that number of cats on each set of two pigs.

Ima Thinker

1. What number of cats will Ima write on

   each set of two pigs? _____

2. How many pigs balance one cow? _____

3. How many cats will balance one cow? _____

4. How did you figure out the answer to #3? _____

_____

Name _____ Date _____

PROBLEM 2

How many pigs will balance one horse?

Toy animals that are the same weigh the same.

I know how many pigs balance 2 goats. I'll write that number of pigs on each set of 2 goats.

Ima Thinker

1. How many goats balance 2 pigs?

_____

2. How many pigs will balance one horse?

_____

3. How did you figure out the answer to #2? _____

_____

4. If one goat weighs 2 pounds, what is the weight of one horse?

_____

Name _____   Date _____

PROBLEM 3

How many rabbits will balance one lamb?

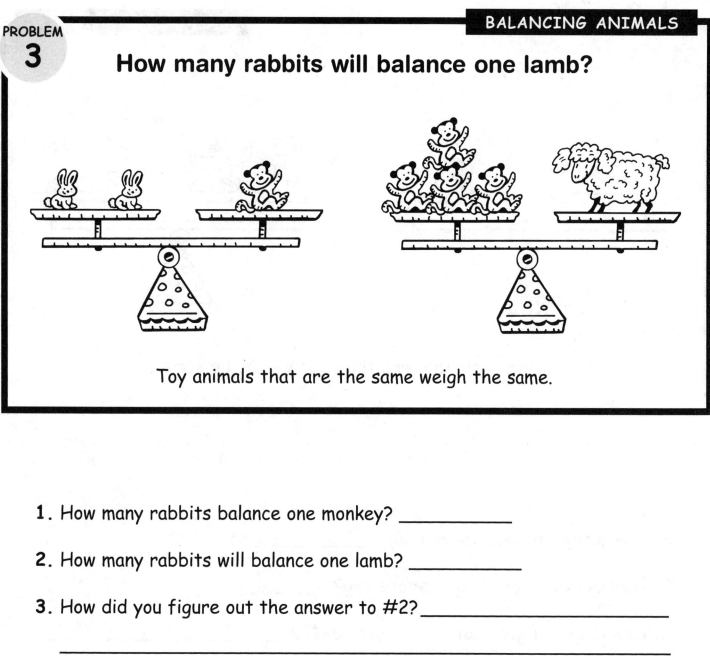

Toy animals that are the same weigh the same.

1. How many rabbits balance one monkey? _____

2. How many rabbits will balance one lamb? _____

3. How did you figure out the answer to #2? _____

_____

4. If one monkey weighs 4 pounds, what is the weight of one lamb?

_____

PROBLEM
4

How many birds will balance one dog?

Toy animals that are the same weigh the same.

1. How many cats balance one dog? _____

2. How many birds will balance one dog? _____

3. How did you figure out the answer to #2? _____

_____

4. If one bird weighs 1 pound, what is the weight of one dog? _____

Math Problem-Solving Packets: Grade 4 © 2012 by Greenes, Findell & Cavanagh, Scholastic Teaching Resources

Name _____ Date _____

PROBLEM
5

How many giraffes will balance one elephant?

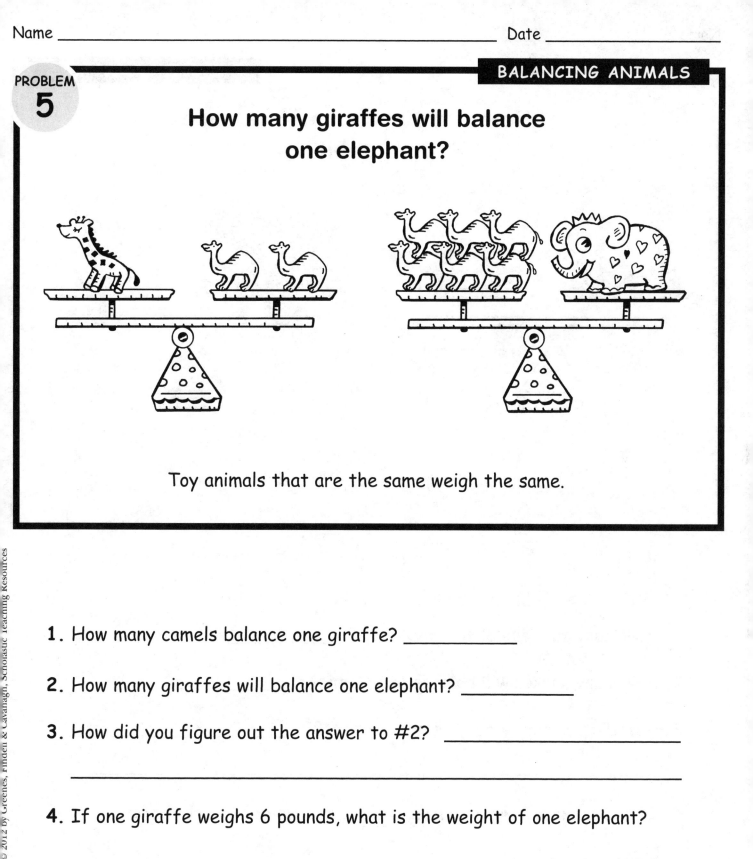

Toy animals that are the same weigh the same.

1. How many camels balance one giraffe? _____

2. How many giraffes will balance one elephant? _____

3. How did you figure out the answer to #2? _____

_____

4. If one giraffe weighs 6 pounds, what is the weight of one elephant?

_____

PROBLEM 6

How many snakes will balance one rabbit?

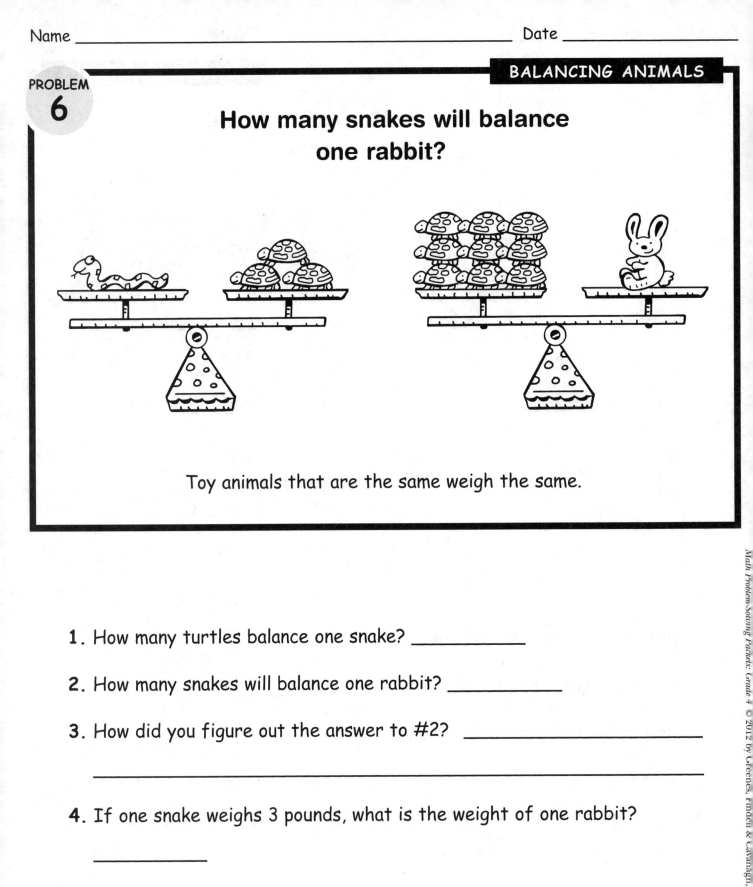

Toy animals that are the same weigh the same.

1. How many turtles balance one snake? _____

2. How many snakes will balance one rabbit? _____

3. How did you figure out the answer to #2? _____

_____

4. If one snake weighs 3 pounds, what is the weight of one rabbit?

_____

Math Problem-Solving Packets: Grade 4 © 2012 by Greenes, Findell & Cavanagh, Scholastic Teaching Resources

PROBLEM 7

How many kittens will balance one puppy?

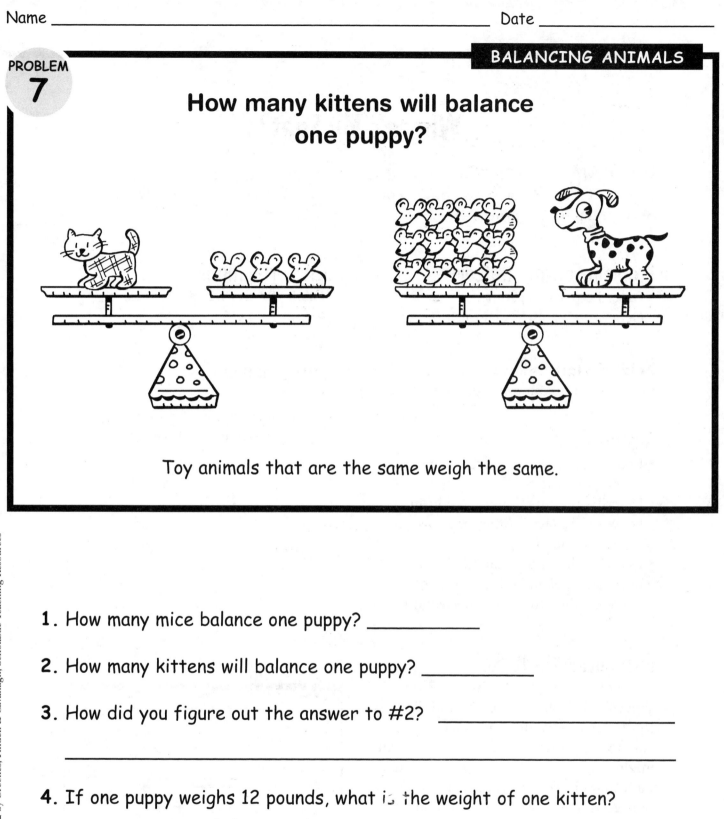

Toy animals that are the same weigh the same.

1. How many mice balance one puppy? _____

2. How many kittens will balance one puppy? _____

3. How did you figure out the answer to #2? _____

_____

4. If one puppy weighs 12 pounds, what is the weight of one kitten?

_____

Math Problem-Solving Packets: Grade 4 © 2012 by Greenes, Findell & Cavanagh, Scholastic Teaching Resources

Where's My Seat?

Overview

Presented with a rectangular array of consecutive numbers, students identify the relationship between row numbers and seat numbers in the rows.

Problem-Solving Strategies

- Describe parts of patterns
- Generalize pattern relationships

Related Math Skill

Compute with counting numbers

Algebra Focus

- Explore variables as representing varying quantities
- Describe the functional relationship between the last number in a row and the row number
- Describe the functional relationship between an element in a row and elements directly above and below it

CCSS Correlations

4.OA.1 • 4.OA.2 • 4.OA.3
4.OA.4 • 4.OA.5

Math Language

- Row
- Spatial terminology: behind, in front of, next to, first (seat), last (seat)

Introducing the Packet

Make photocopies of "Solve the Problem: Where's My Seat?" (page 66) and distribute to students. Have students work in pairs, encouraging them to discuss strategies they might use to solve the problem. You may want to walk around and listen in on some of their discussions. After a few minutes, display the problem on the interactive whiteboard (see the CD) and use the following questions to guide a whole-class discussion on how to solve the problem:

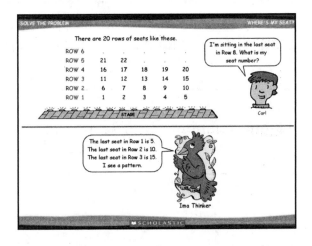

- What is the last number in Row 1? *(5)* Row 2? *(10)* Row 5? *(25)*

- How can you figure out the last number in a row? *(Count the row numbers by 5s or multiply 5 x row number)*

- What is Carl's seat number? *(40)* How do you know? *(The last number of Row 8 is 5 x 8, or 40)*

- Where is Alphonse sitting? *(First seat in Row 10)* How can you figure out the number of the first seat in Row 10? *(It is one more than the last seat in Row 9, or 5 x 9 + 1 = 46)*

- What is Peter's seat number? *(41)* How did you figure it out? *(46 – 5 = 41)*

Work together as a class to answer the questions in "Solve the Problem: Where's My Seat?"

Math Chat With "Make the Case"

Display "Make the Case: Where's My Seat?" on the interactive whiteboard. Before students can decide which character is "sharp as a tack," they need to figure out the answer to the problem. Encourage students to work in pairs to solve the problem. Then bring the class together for another whole-class discussion. Ask:

- Who has the right answer? *(Marlee Marlin)*

- How did you figure it out? *(The last seat in Row 7 is 70. The first seat in Row 8 is 71. The seat next to 71 is 72.)*

- How do you think Wally Walrus got the answer 82? *(He probably thought that all of the seats in Row 8 have numbers in the 80s. So the first seat is 81 and the one next to it is 81 + 1, or 82.)*

- How do you think Ralph Rhino got the answer 71? *(He probably didn't read the whole problem. He got the number of the first seat of the row, but forgot to get the number of the seat next to the first seat.)*

SOLVE THE PROBLEM

WHERE'S MY SEAT?

There are 20 rows of seats like these.

ROW 6	.	.	.	.	.
ROW 5	21	22	.	.	.
ROW 4	16	17	18	19	20
ROW 3	11	12	13	14	15
ROW 2	6	7	8	9	10
ROW 1	1	2	3	4	5

STAGE

I'm sitting in the last seat in Row 8. What is my seat number?

Carl

The last seat in Row 1 is 5.
The last seat in Row 2 is 10.
The last seat in Row 3 is 15.
I see a pattern.

Ima Thinker

1. What pattern did Ima see? _____

_____

2. Carl is in seat _____ .

3. Alphonse is sitting in the first seat in Row 10. Alphonse is in seat

_____ .

4. Peter is sitting in the seat right in front of Alphonse.

Peter is in seat _____ .

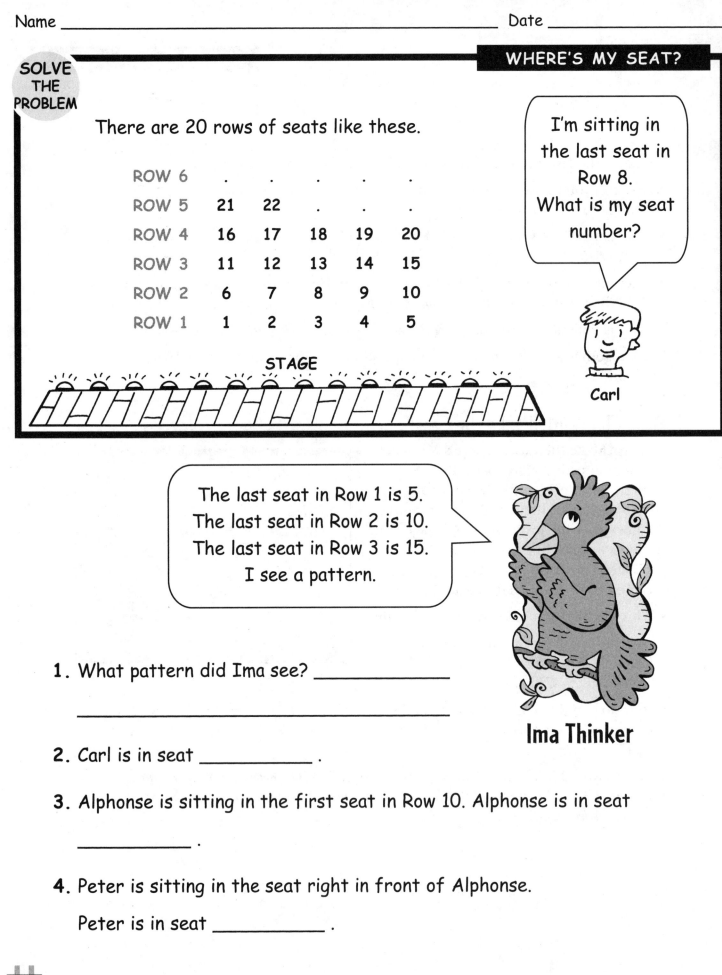

Math Problem-Solving Packets: Grade 4 © 2012 by Greenes, Findell & Cavanagh, Scholastic Teaching Resources

Name _____   Date _____

MAKE THE CASE

I'm sitting in Row 8. My seat is next to the first seat in the row. What is my seat number?

Olivia

There are 10 rows of seats like these.

ROW 5	.	.	.	.	.	.	.	.	.	.
ROW 4	31	32	.	.	.	.	.	.	.	.
ROW 3	21	22	23	24	25	26	27	28	29	30
ROW 2	11	12	13	14	15	16	17	18	19	20
ROW 1	1	2	3	4	5	6	7	8	9	10

STAGE

That's easy. She is in seat 82.

72 is the right answer. I just know it.

Marlee Marlin

No way. It has to be seat 71.

Wally Walrus

Ralph Rhino

Who is sharp as a tack?

Math Problem-Solving Packets: Grade 4 © 2012 by Greenes, Findell & Cavanagh, Scholastic Teaching Resources

PROBLEM 1

There are 20 rows of seats like these.

ROW 6	.	.	.	.
ROW 5	17	18	.	.
ROW 4	13	14	15	16
ROW 3	9	10	11	12
ROW 2	5	6	7	8
ROW 1	1	2	3	4

STAGE

I'm sitting in the last seat in Row 6.
What is my seat number?

Jeffrey

The last seat in Row 1 is 4.
The last seat in Row 2 is 8.
The last seat in Row 3 is 12.
I see a pattern.

Ima Thinker

1. What pattern did Ima see? _____

_____

2. Jeffrey is in seat _____ .

3. Frida is sitting right behind Jeffrey. Frida is in seat _____ .

4. Theo is sitting next to Frida. Theo is in seat _____ .

Math Problem-Solving Packets: Grade 4 © 2012 by Greenes, Findell & Cavanagh, Scholastic Teaching Resources

PROBLEM 2

There are 20 rows of seats like these.

ROW 6	.	.	.
ROW 5	13	14	.
ROW 4	10	11	12
ROW 3	7	8	9
ROW 2	4	5	6
ROW 1	1	2	3

STAGE

I'm sitting in the last seat in Row 9. What is my seat number?

Penny

The last seat in Row 1 is 3.
The last seat in Row 2 is 6.
The last seat in Row 3 is 9.
I see a pattern.

Ima Thinker

1. What pattern did Ima see? _____

_____

2. Penny is in seat _____ .

3. Zach is sitting next to Penny. Zach is in seat _____ .

4. Felipe is sitting right in front of Zach. Felipe is in seat _____ .

WHERE'S MY SEAT?

There are 20 rows of seats like these.

ROW 5	33	34	.	.	.	.	.	.
ROW 4	25	26	27	28	29	30	31	32
ROW 3	17	18	19	20	21	22	23	24
ROW 2	9	10	11	12	13	14	15	16
ROW 1	1	2	3	4	5	6	7	8

STAGE

I'm sitting in the last seat in Row 10.
What is my seat number?

Jeremy

The last seat in Row 1 is 8.
The last seat in Row 2 is 16.
The last seat in Row 3 is 24.
I see a pattern.

Ima Thinker

1. What pattern did Ima see? _____
_____

2. Jeremy is sitting in seat _____ .

3. Dina is sitting next to Jeremy. Dina is in seat _____ .

4. Logan is sitting in the first seat in Row 10. Logan is in seat
_____ .

Math Problem-Solving Packets: Grade 4 © 2012 by Greenes, Findell & Cavanagh, Scholastic Teaching Resources

PROBLEM 4

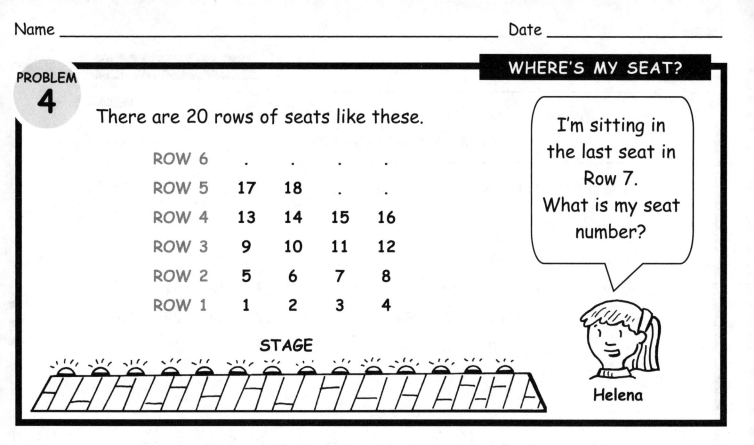

There are 20 rows of seats like these.

ROW 6	.	.	.	.
ROW 5	17	18	.	.
ROW 4	13	14	15	16
ROW 3	9	10	11	12
ROW 2	5	6	7	8
ROW 1	1	2	3	4

STAGE

I'm sitting in the last seat in Row 7. What is my seat number?

Helena

1. Helena is sitting in seat _____ .

2. Ginny is sitting in the first seat in Row 7. Ginny is in seat _____ .

3. Tomas is sitting right in front of Ginny. Tomas is in Row _____ and his seat number is _____ .

4. Leo is sitting right in front of Tomas. Leo is in Row _____ and his seat number is _____ .

Math Problem-Solving Packets: Grade 4 © 2012 by Greenes, Findell & Cavanagh, Scholastic Teaching Resources

PROBLEM 5

> My seat is next to the last seat of Row 7.
> What is my seat number?

Stefan

There are 20 rows of seats like these.

ROW 6	.	.	.	.	.	.	.	.	.	.
ROW 5	41	42	.	.	.	.	.	.	.	.
ROW 4	31	32	33	34	35	36	37	38	39	40
ROW 3	21	22	23	24	25	26	27	28	29	30
ROW 2	11	12	13	14	15	16	17	18	19	20
ROW 1	1	2	3	4	5	6	7	8	9	10

STAGE

1. Stefan is sitting in seat _____.

2. A.J. sat two rows directly in front of Stefan. A.J. sat in Row _____

   and seat _____.

3. Charlie sat in seat 93. Charlie was in Row _____.

4. How did you figure out Charlie's row number? _____

   _____

Math Problem-Solving Packets: Grade 4 © 2012 by Greenes, Findell & Cavanagh, Scholastic Teaching Resources

Name _____ Date _____

PROBLEM
6

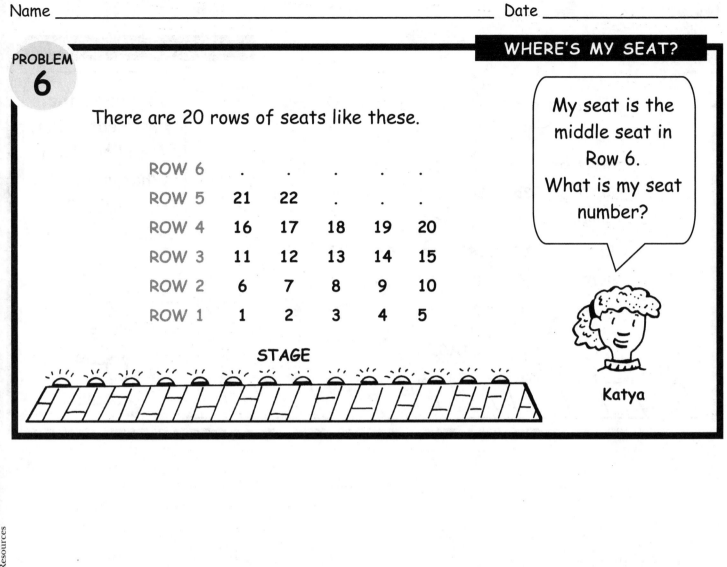

There are 20 rows of seats like these.

ROW 6	.	.	.	.	.
ROW 5	21	22	.	.	.
ROW 4	16	17	18	19	20
ROW 3	11	12	13	14	15
ROW 2	6	7	8	9	10
ROW 1	1	2	3	4	5

STAGE

My seat is the middle seat in Row 6. What is my seat number?

Katya

1. Katya is sitting in seat _____.

2. Doug sat directly behind Katya. Doug is in Row _____ and seat _____.

3. Jimmy sat two rows directly behind Doug. Jimmy is in Row _____ and seat _____.

4. How did you figure out Jimmy's seat number? _____

_____

Name _____ Date _____

PROBLEM 7

There are 20 rows of seats like these.

ROW 6	.	.	.	.	.	.
ROW 5	25	26	.	.	.	.
ROW 4	19	20	21	22	23	24
ROW 3	13	14	15	16	17	18
ROW 2	7	8	9	10	11	12
ROW 1	1	2	3	4	5	6

STAGE

> I'll go to the first seat in Row 9 and sit down. What is my seat number?

Stella

1. Stella is sitting at seat _____.

2. Ally sat right next to Stella. Ally is in seat _____.

3. Samantha sat right in front of Ally. Samantha is in Row _____ and seat _____.

4. How did you figure out Samantha's seat number? _____

_____

Math Problem-Solving Packets: Grade 4 © 2012 by Greenes, Findell & Cavanagh, Scholastic Teaching Resources

SOLVE
IT

1. **Look**   What is the problem?

2. **Plan and Do**   What will you do first? How will you solve the problem?

3. **Answer and Check**   How can you be sure your answer is correct?

SOLVE IT: DOG DATA

How much is each dog's doctor bill?

Spot   Windy Day   DeVine   Holly Wood

Use the facts to figure out the doctor's bill for each dog.

FACTS:

Ⓐ Spot's bill was twice as much as Windy Day's bill.

Ⓑ Windy Day's bill was $50 more than DeVine's bill.

Ⓒ DeVine's bill was $\frac{1}{3}$ of Holly Wood's bill.

Ⓓ Holly Wood's bill was $30.

- -

SOLVE IT: STAMP STUMPERS

How much is one cone stamp?

The total cost of the four stamps on the envelope is 49¢.

The cone stamps cost the same.

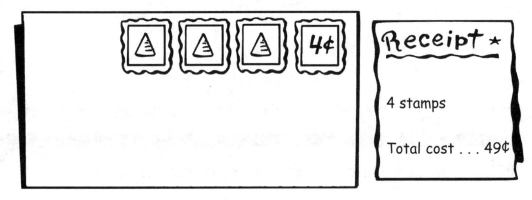

SOLVE IT: JERSEY NUMBER

What is the number on the player's jersey?

The letter **K** stands for the number on the jersey.

Use the clues to figure out **K**.

CLUES:

1) $2 \times K > 18$

2) 4 is a factor of **K**

3) The tens digit is one more than the ones digit

4) $K < 100 - 60$

SOLVE IT: WEIGH IN

How much does Maria the pig weigh?

Scale A

Scale B

Scale C

How many monkeys will balance one elephant?

Toy animals that are the same weigh the same.

SOLVE IT: WHERE'S MY SEAT?

> Henry is sitting in the first seat in Row 7. I'm sitting next to Henry. What's my seat number?

Kayla

There are 20 rows of seats like these.

ROW 4	28	.	.	.	.	.	.	.	.
ROW 3	19	20	21	22	23	24	25	26	27
ROW 2	10	11	12	13	14	15	16	17	18
ROW 1	1	2	3	4	5	6	7	8	9

STAGE

ANSWER KEY

Dog Data (pages 11–19)
Solve the Problem
1. Fact C
2. 12
3. 15
4. Work backward. Fact C: Holly Wood is 6 years old. Fact B: Ms. Clean is 2 x 6, or 12 years old. Fact A: Popeye is 12 + 3, or 15 years old.

Make the Case
Who is sharp as a tack?
Marlee Marlin

Problem 1
1. Fact C
2. 7 years old
3. 2 years old
4. Work backward. Fact C: Bubba is 14 years old. Fact B: DeVine is ½ of 14, or 7 years old. Fact A. Howdy is 7 – 5, or 2 years old.

Problem 2
1. Fact D
2. 48 pounds
3. 38 pounds
4. Work backward. Fact D: Windy Day weighs 24 pounds. Fact C: Dandy weighs 2 x 24, or 48 pounds. Fact B: Bubba weighs 48 – 10, or 38 pounds. Fact A: Melody weighs 38 – 4, or 34 pounds.

Problem 3
1. Fact D
2. 50 pounds
3. 25 pounds
4. Work backward. Fact D: Madam Peppy weighs 5 pounds. Fact C: DeVine weighs 10 x 5, or 50 pounds. Fact B: Popeye is ½ of 50, or 25 pounds. Fact A: Spot is 25 – 4, or 21 pounds.

Problem 4
1. Fact D
2. 38 pounds
3. 55 pounds
4. Work backward. Fact D: Ms. Clean weighs 19 pounds. Fact C: Holly Wood weighs 2 x 19, or 38 pounds. Fact B: Howdy weighs 38 + 17, or 55 pounds. Fact A: Betsy weighs 55 – 10, or 45 pounds.

Problem 5
1. Fact D
2. 9 ounces
3. 17 ounces
4. Work backward. Fact D: Howdy eats 18 ounces of food. Fact C: Ms. Clean eats ½ x 18, or 9 ounces. Fact B: Dandy eats 9 + 8, or 17 ounces. Fact A: Spot eats 17 – 2, or 15 ounces.

Problem 6
1. Fact D
2. 12 ounces
3. 3 ounces
4. Work backward. Fact D: Windy Day eats 8 ounces of food. Fact C: Popeye eats 20 – 8, or 12 ounces. Fact B: Madam Peppy eats ¼ of 12, or 3 ounces. Fact A: Melody eats 6 + 3, or 9 ounces.

Problem 7
1. Fact D
2. $80
3. $90
4. Work backward. Fact D: Ms. Clean's bill was $40. Fact C: Madam Peppy's bill was 2 x $40, or $80. Fact B: Dandy's bill was $80 + $10, or $90. Fact A: Betsy's bill was $150 – $90, or $60.

Solve It: Dog Data
1. Look: Facts are given about the doctor bills for four dogs. Fact D about Holly Wood's bill is the only cost known. To figure out DeVine's bill, we need to use Holly Wood's bill. For Windy Day's bill, we need to know DeVine's bill. For Spot's bill, we need to know Windy Day's bill
2. Plan and Do: Work backward. Fact D: Holly Wood's bill was $30. Fact C: DeVine's bill was ⅓ of $30, or $10. Fact B: Windy Day's bill was $50 + $10, or $60. Fact A: Spot's bill was 2 x $60, or $120.
3. Answer and Check: Spot's bill was $120, Windy Day's bill was $60, DeVine's bill was $20, and Holly Wood's bill was $30. To check, use the amounts of the bills for each dog and check against the facts. Do they make sense? DeVine's bill: $10, which is ⅓ of Holly Wood's $30 bill. Windy Day's bill: $60, which is $50 more than DeVine's bill of $10. Spot's bill: $120, which is 2 x Windy Day's $60 bill.

Stamp Stumpers (pages 22–30)
Solve the Problem
1. By taking away the 5¢ stamp from the envelope and subtracting 5¢ from the total cost, the amount left would be the cost of the four chevron stamps
2. 13¢ – 5¢ = 8¢
3. 2¢
4. When you take away the 5¢ stamp, the total cost changes to 13¢ – 5¢, or 8¢. So the four chevron stamps cost 8¢. One chevron stamp is 8¢ ÷ 4, or 2¢.

Make the Case
Who is sharp as a tack? Ralph Rhino

Problem 1
1. By taking the 2¢ stamp off the envelope and subtracting 2¢ from the total cost, the amount left is the cost of the three octagon stamps.
2. 17¢ – 2¢ = 15¢
3. 5¢
4. When you take away the 2¢ stamp, the total cost changes to 17¢ – 2¢, or 15¢. So the three octagon stamps cost 15¢. That means that one octagon stamp is 15¢ ÷ 3, or 5¢.

Problem 2
1. By taking the 3¢ stamp off the envelope and subtracting 3¢ from the total cost, the amount left is the cost of the three pentagon stamps.
2. 10¢
3. 33¢ – 3¢ = 30¢; 30¢ ÷ 3 = 10¢
4. 30¢

Problem 3
1. By taking the 8¢ stamp off the envelope and subtracting 8¢ from the total cost, the number left is the cost of the three triangle stamps.
2. 7¢
3. 29¢ – 8 = 21¢; 21¢ ÷ 3 = 7¢
4. 30¢

Problem 4
1. 6¢
2. 25¢ – 1¢ = 24¢; 24¢ ÷ 4 = 6¢
3. 20¢
4. 8¢

Problem 5
1. 3¢
2. 15¢ – 3¢ = 12¢; 12¢ ÷ 4 = 3¢
3. 16¢
4. 5¢

Problem 6
1. 8¢
2. 31¢ – 2¢ – 5¢ = 24¢; 24¢ ÷ 3 = 8¢
3. 28¢
4. 9¢

Problem 7
1. 9¢
2. 40¢ – 4¢ = 36¢; 36¢ ÷ 4 = 9¢
3. 47¢
4. 20¢

Solve It: Stamp Stumpers
1. Look: There are four stamps on the envelope and a receipt that shows the total cost of 49¢. There are three cone stamps and one 4¢ stamp. The problem is to figure out the cost of one cone stamp.
2. Plan and Do: First, pretend to take the 4¢ stamp off the envelope and subtract 4¢ from the total cost. That means that the cost of the three cone stamps is 49¢ – 4¢, or 45¢. Divide 45¢ by 3 to get the value of one cone stamp.
3. Answer and Check: Each stamp is 45¢ ÷ 3, or 15¢. To check, record 15¢ on each cone and add the costs: 15¢ + 4¢ + 15¢ + 15¢ = 49¢. This sum matches the total cost.

Jersey Number (pages 33–41)
Solve the Problem
1. 9, 8, 7, 6, 5, 4, 3, 2, 1, and 0
2. A = 8
3. Possible answer: From Clue 1, A is 9 or less. Make a list of those numbers. Clue 2 eliminates 0 through 5, leaving 6, 7, 8, and 9. Clue 3 eliminates 7 and 9, leaving 6 and 8. Clue 4 eliminates 6. So, A is 8.
4. Replace A with 8. Check 8 with each clue: 8 + 8 < 20, 8 > 5, 2 is a factor of 8, and 3 is not a factor of 8.

Make the Case
Who is sharp as a tack? Wally Walrus

Problem 1
1. Clue 1 gives the greatest number that C can be. C is 15 or less.
2. C = 3
3. Possible answer: Clue 1 gives the list of numbers 0 through 15. Clue 2 eliminates all even numbers. Clue 3 eliminates 5 and 15. Clue 4 eliminates all numbers except for 3 and 9. Clue 5 eliminates 9. So, C is 3.
4. Replace C with 3. Check 3 with each clue.

Problem 2
1. Clue 4 gives the greatest number that D can be. D is 17 or less.
2. D = 15
3. Possible answer: Clue 4 gives D as 17 or less. List the numbers 0 through 17. Clue 2 eliminates zero through 5. Clue 3 eliminates all even numbers. Clue 1 eliminates 7, 11, 13, and 17. Clue 5 eliminates 9. So, D is 15.
4. Replace D with 15. Check 15 with each clue.

Problem 3
1. Clue 3 gives the greatest number that E can be. E is 7 or less.
2. E = 7
3. Possible answer: Clue 3 gives the list of numbers 0 through 7. Clue 1 eliminates 0, 1, and 2. Clue 2 eliminates 4 and 6. Clue 4 eliminates 3. Clue 5 eliminates 5. So, E is 7.
4. Replace E with 7. Check 7 with each clue.

Problem 4
1. Clue 1 gives the greatest number that F can be. F is 9 or less.
2. F = 8
3. Possible answer: Clue 1 gives the list of numbers 0 through 9. Clue 2 eliminates all numbers less than 5. Clue 3 eliminates all odd numbers. Clue 4 eliminates 6. So, F is 8.
4. Replace F with 8. Check 8 with each clue.

Problem 5
1. Clue 2 gives the greatest number that G can be. G is 29 or less.
2. G = 21
3. Possible answer: Clue 2 gives the list of numbers 0 through 29. Clue 1 eliminates all numbers 20 and less. Clue 3 eliminates all even numbers. Clue 4 eliminates all numbers except for 21 and 27. Clue 5 eliminates 27. So, G is 21.
4. Replace G with 21. Check 21 with each clue.

Problem 6
1. Clue 4 gives the greatest number that H can be. H is 19 or less.
2. H = 12
3. Possible answer: Clue 4 gives the list of numbers 0 through 19. Clue 1 eliminates all numbers 10 and less. Clue 3 eliminates all odd numbers. Clue 2 eliminates 14 and 16. Clue 5 eliminates 18. So, H is 12.
4. Replace H with 12. Check 12 with each clue.

Problem 7
1. Clue 2 gives the greatest number that J can be. J is 39 or less.
2. J = 35
3. Possible answer: Clue 2 gives the list of numbers 0 through 39. Clue 1 eliminates all numbers 20 and less. Clue 4 eliminates all numbers except for 25, 30, and 35. Clue 3 eliminates 30. Clue 5 eliminates 25. So, J is 35.
4. Replace J with 35. Check 35 with each clue.

Solve It: Jersey Number

1. Look: Four clues are given to figure out the number on the player's jersey. The number is represented by the letter K.

2. Plan and Do: Clues 1 and 4 establish the range for K. K > 9 and K < 40, so K can be any number 10 through 39. Clue 2 indicates that 4 is a factor of K, so eliminate all numbers except for 12, 16, 20, 24, 28, 32, and 36. The only number that fits Clue 3 is 32. So, K is 32.

3. Answer and Check: K = 32. Replace K with 32. Check 32 with each clue.

Weigh In (pages 44–52)
Solve the Problem

1. 85
2. 40
3. 15
4. Answers will vary. Possible answer: On scale B, Tom weighs 85 pounds. On scale A, Tom and Smudge weigh 100 pounds altogether. So Smudge weighs 100 – 85, or 15 pounds.

Make the Case

Who is sharp as a tack? Ralph Rhino

Problem 1
1. 7
2. 8
3. 65
4. 80 pounds

Problem 2
1. 67
2. 43
3. 4
4. 24 pounds

Problem 3
1. 80
2. 75
3. 40
4. 195

Problem 4
1. 18
2. 90
3. 10
4. 8 pounds

Problem 5
1. 12
2. 13
3. 7
4. Answers may vary. Possible answer: The cage and Tabby are 25 pounds. Winslow weighs 32 – 25, or 7 pounds.

Problem 6
1. 15
2. 35
3. 70
4. Answers may vary. Possible answer: Bowser and one bag of food weigh 50 pounds on scale A. Since Bowser and one bag of food is 50 pounds, then on scale B, Mario is 120 – 50, or 70 pounds.

Problem 7
1. 10
2. 9
3. 14
4. Answers may vary. Possible answer: On scale B, one box of cat litter is 20 ÷ 2, or 10 pounds. On scale C, one bag of cat food is 27 ÷ 3, or 9 pounds. On scale A, the box of cat litter and the bag of cat food are 10 + 9, or 19 pounds. So, El Gato the cat is 33 – 19, or 14 pounds.

Solve It: Weigh In

1. Look: Three scales A, B, and C. On A, Peter and one box of dog bones are 66 pounds. On B, Peter and Maria the pig are 77 pounds. On C, 3 boxes of dog bones are 18 pounds. The problem is to figure out how much Maria weighs.

2. Plan and Do: On scale C, one box of dog bones is 18 ÷ 3, or 6 pounds. On scale A, the box of dog bones is 6 pounds, so Peter is 66 – 6, or 60 pounds. On scale B, since Peter is 60 pounds, then Maria the pig is 77 – 60, or 17 pounds.

3. Answer and Check: Maria is 17 pounds. To check, replace each box of dog bones with 6 pounds, Peter with 60 pounds, and Maria with 17 pounds, and figure out the sum of the weight on each scale. The sums should match the numbers of pounds shown on the scales.

Balancing Animals (pages 55–63)
Solve the Problem

1. 2 fish
2. 3 frogs
3. 6 fish
4. Two fish balance 1 frog, so 6 fish will balance 3 frogs. That means 6 fish will balance 1 shark.

Make the Case

Who is sharp as a tack? Wally Walrus

Problem 1
1. 1 cat
2. 4 pigs
3. 2 cats
4. One cat balances 2 pigs, so 2 cats will balance 4 pigs. That means 2 cats will balance 1 cow.

Problem 2
1. 2 goats
2. 4 pigs
3. Two goats balance 2 pigs, so 4 goats will balance 4 pigs. That means 4 pigs will balance 1 horse.
4. 8 pounds

Problem 3
1. 2 rabbits
2. 8 rabbits
3. Two rabbits balance 1 monkey, so 8 rabbits will balance 4 monkeys. That means 8 rabbits will balance 1 lamb.
4. 16 pounds

Problem 4
1. 3 cats
2. 12 birds
3. Four birds balance 1 cat, so 12 birds will balance 3 cats. That means 12 birds will balance one dog.
4. 12 pounds

Problem 5
1. 2 camels
2. 3 giraffes
3. One giraffe balances 2 camels, so 3 giraffes will balance 6 camels. That means 3 giraffes will balance one elephant.
4. 18 pounds

Problem 6
1. 3 turtles
2. 3 snakes
3. One snake balances 3 turtles, so 3 snakes will balance 9 turtles. That means 3 snakes will balance 1 rabbit.
4. 9 pounds

Problem 7
1. 12 mice
2. 4 kittens
3. Three mice balance 1 kitten, so 12 mice will balance 4 kittens. That means 4 kittens will balance 1 puppy.
4. 3 pounds

Solve It: Balancing Animals

1. Look: There are two pan balances. On the first pan balance, 2 monkeys balance 1 lion. On the second pan balance, 5 lions balance 1 elephant. The problem is to figure out how many monkeys will balance one elephant.

2. Plan and Do: One lion balances 2 monkeys, so 5 lions will balance 10 monkeys. That means 10 monkeys will balance 1 elephant.

3. Answer and Check: 10 monkeys will balance one elephant. To check, write the number of monkeys on each lion and count the monkeys. There should be 10.

Where's My Seat? (pages 66–74)
Solve the Problem

1. The number of the last seat in a row is 5 times the row number.
2. 40
3. 46
4. 41

Make the Case

Who is sharp as a tack?
Marlee Marlin

Problem 1
1. The number of the last seat in a row is 4 times the row number.
2. 24
3. 28
4. 27

Problem 2
1. The number of the last seat in a row is 3 times the row number.
2. 27
3. 26
4. 23

Problem 3
1. The number of the last seat in a row is 8 times the row number.
2. 80
3. 79
4. 73

Problem 4
1. 28
2. 25
3. Row 6 and seat 21
4. Row 5 and seat 17

Problem 5
1. 69
2. Row 5 and seat 49
3. Row 10
4. Answers may vary. Possible answer: The last seat in Row 9 is 9 x 10, or 90. So, 93 is in row 10.

Problem 6
1. 28
2. Row 7 and seat 33
3. Row 9 and seat 43
4. Answers may vary. Possible answer: Katya is in Row 6 and seat 28. Doug is in Row 7 and seat 28 + 5, or 33. Jimmy is in Row 9 and in seat 33 + 5 + 5, or 43.

Problem 7
1. 49
2. 50
3. Row 8 and seat 44
4. Answers may vary. Possible answer: The last number in Row 8 is 8 x 6, or 48. Stella is in 48 + 1, or seat 49 in Row 9. Ally is in seat 49 + 1, or 50. Samantha is in Row 8 and seat 50 – 6, or 44.

Solve It: Where's My Seat?

1. Look: Rows of numbers with 9 numbers in each row. The last number in each row is a multiple of 9 and is 9 x the row number. The problem is to figure out Kayla's seat number.

2. Plan and Do: First figure out where Henry is sitting. The number of the last seat in Row 6 is 6 x 9, or 54. The first seat in Row 7 is 54 + 1, or 55 so Henry is in seat 55. Kayla is in seat 55 + 1, or 56.

3. Answer & Check: The answer is 56. To check, use a different solution method. The last seat in Row 7 is 7 x 9, or 63. There are 9 seats in a row. Count backward from 63 to the first seat in the row, 55. Then the seat next to the first seat is 56.